Helping Children
with Feelings

Helping Children
with Low
Self-Esteem

Ruby and the
Rubbish Bin

CU00924165

A Guidebook

Margot Sunderland

Illustrated by

Nicky Armstrong

Speechmark

Speechmark Publishing Ltd
Telford Road, Bicester, Oxon OX26 4LQ, UK

Note on the Text

For the sake of clarity alone, throughout the text the child has been referred to as 'he' and the parent as 'she'.

Unless otherwise stated, for clarity alone, where 'mummy', 'mother' or 'mother figure' is used, this refers to either parent or other primary caretaker.

Confidentiality

Where appropriate, full permission has been granted by adults, or children and their parents, to use clinical material. Other illustrations comprise synthesised and disguised examples to ensure anonymity.

Published by
Speechmark Publishing Ltd, Telford Road, Bicester, Oxon OX26 4LQ, UK
Tel: +44 (0) 1869 244644   Fax: +44 (0) 1869 320040
www.speechmark.net

First published 2003
Reprinted 2004, 2005

002-5153/Printed in the United Kingdom/1010

British Library Cataloguing in Publication Data
Sunderland, Margot
   Helping children with low self-esteem – (Helping children with feelings)
   1. Self-esteem in children 2. Emotional problems of children
   3. Problem children – behaviour modification
   I. Title II. Armstrong, Nicky
   155.4'5124

ISBN 0 86388 466 0

Contents

This book is accompanied by the childrens' story book, *Ruby and the Rubbish Bin* by Margot Sunderland.

About the Author

MARGOT SUNDERLAND is a registered Child Therapeutic Counsellor, Supervisor and Trainer (UKATC), and a registered Integrative Arts Psychotherapist (UKCP). She is Chair of the Children and Young People section of The United Kingdom Association for Therapeutic Counselling.

Margot is also Principal of the Institute for Arts in Therapy and Education – a recognised fully accredited Higher Education College running Masters Degree courses in Integrative Child Psychotherapy and Arts Psychotherapy. She was founder of the project 'Helping where it Hurts', which offers free therapy and counselling to troubled children in several primary schools in North London.

Margot is a published poet and author of *Choreographing the Stage Musical* (Routledge Theatre Arts, New York and J Garnet Miller, England); *Draw on Your Emotions* (Speechmark Publishing, Bicester and Erickson, Italy); *Using Storytelling as a Therapeutic Tool for Children* (Speechmark Publishing, Bicester, awarded Highly Commended in the Mental Health category of the 2002 BMA Medical Book Competition), and the acclaimed *Helping Children with Feelings* series of storybooks and handbooks (Speechmark Publishing, Bicester).

About the Illustrator

NICKY ARMSTRONG holds an MA from the Slade School of Fine Art and a BA Hons in Theatre Design from the University of Central England. She is currently teacher of trompe l'œil at The Hampstead School of Decorative Arts, London. She has achieved major commissions nationally and internationally in mural work and fine art.

INTRODUCTION

Who this book will help

☆ Children who don't like themselves.

☆ Children who have known too much discouragement.

☆ Children who have been deeply shamed.

☆ Children who have received too much criticism in their life.

☆ Children who feel there is something fundamentally wrong with them – for example, that they are ugly, smelly, stupid.

☆ Children who let people treat them badly because they feel they don't deserve better.

☆ Children who do not accept praise or appreciation because they feel they don't deserve it.

☆ Children who feel defeated by life.

☆ Children who feel that they are fundamentally unimportant.

☆ Children who feel unwanted or unlovable.

☆ Children who bully because they think they are worthless.

☆ Children who think they are worthless because they are bullied.

☆ Children who feel they don't belong.

☆ Children who haven't been encouraged enough in their lives.

☆ Children who do not seek friends because they think no-one would want to be their friend.

WHAT LIFE IS LIKE FOR CHILDREN WHO THINK THEY ARE WORTHLESS

We can find a lot of different ways to express how much we hate ourselves. (Williamson, 1992)

When you feel worthless, life can lose its magic and end up a pretty miserable affair

For children who think they are worthless, life can all too easily lose its magic, its fascination and excitement. Rather, each day can be met with the anticipation of further disappointment, failure, feelings of inadequacy, and a sense that something is fundamentally wrong with you. So children who don't like themselves often have too little hope. This can have a terrible wearing-down effect, draining the child's natural resources of energy and enthusiasm.

When a child thinks he is worthless, he can start to retreat from life. He can place himself on the outside, because he doesn't feel 'good enough'. He may also dislike his own company because of his self-criticism or self-hate. He may believe that anything he does will also be worthless – for example, school-work, anything he makes, says, sings, invents, or dreams of. As a result, he can give up too easily, or not start something in the first place. This is in contrast to a child with high self-esteem who will start something, experiment, then persevere and often triumph in the face of adversity.

Feeling worthless can also blight a child's moment-to-moment perception, just as real rubbish can pollute the physical environment and spoil the view as far as the eye can see. So the world and life itself become drab, something to get through and without allure.

> Garbage… is believable enough
> to get our attention, getting in the way, piling
> up, stinking, turning brooks brownish and
> creamy white…
>
> (Ammons, 1993, p18)

Statements made in play therapy by children aged 4–10 with very low self-esteem

☆ 'This story is about a little girl who drowned. The Mummy could have saved her but she didn't because the little girl wasn't pretty enough. The little girl didn't really want to live any more.' (Story by Tracey, aged six.)

☆ 'Sometimes I feel like a sort of insect under people's feet, a very miserable insect actually.' (Angus, aged eight.)

☆ 'I never seem to get listened to. I think it's because what I say is not worth hearing.' (Dawn, aged ten.)

Going unnoticed, and not belonging

'Can you lay eggs?' asked the hen. 'No? Then kindly keep your views to yourself!' The cat asked, 'Can you arch your back and purr, or give out sparks? No? Then you had better keep quiet while sensible people are talking.' So the [ugly] duckling sat in a corner and moped. (Andersen, 1994)

Some children who feel worthless will not speak in company, believing that 'What I have to say isn't really worth hearing', or because they fear that if they did speak out they would be criticised. Their self-imposed silence or reticence can simply confirm their belief in their lack of self-worth, as they are then often forgotten or ignored. In contrast, time and time again, they bear painful witness to those in a group who *do* have a voice, and who *are* heard. If this continues, the child can move through life with a sense of 'facelessness' and voicelessness in their self-presentation. Hence many children with low self-worth are those in the classroom that no-one seems to notice or remember – those children characterised by 'a sense of not really being a person at all' (Hinshelwood, 1989, p187).

Some fairy stories speak of the 'quiet unnoticed' child, voiceless and faceless. An example is the Tin Soldier in *The Steadfast Tin Soldier*:

> Although they were almost treading on the soldier they somehow failed to see him. If he had called out, 'Here I am!' they would have found him easily, but he didn't think it proper behaviour to cry out when he was in uniform. (Andersen, 1996)

How feelings of worthlessness can make a child wish he were dead

> Vile worm, thou wast o'erlooked even in thy birth.
> (Shakespeare, *The Merry Wives of Windsor* 5 (5), p82)

A vivid example of this was a boy who felt so worthless that he went around calling himself 'Little Shit' (this was what his stepfather often called him). When he saw himself in photographs he would burn out his face with a cigarette, believing that his face spoilt the picture. When asked what he wanted to do when he grew up, he said in complete seriousness that he wanted to work down a sewer. When he was 16 he tried to take his own life – he had so totally identified with the 'Little Shit' image.

How praise can have no effect and success can be painful

> If you put a diamond collar on a dog it's still a dog, made more ludicrous by the diamonds around its neck. (Keenan, 1992, p167)

If a child doubts his own worth, then any praise or encouragement may seem false, plain inaccurate, or even ridiculous. This stems from a deeply-held belief that, 'Praise does not fit with the person I know I am inside.' Such children may contend that any compliments they get are worthless since they are not true: the person is simply humouring, pitying or wanting something from them.

When children 'know' they are rubbish, tragically often very little will penetrate such a fixed and deeply ingrained view. This can be extremely exasperating for the person giving the very genuine praise, who then in turn feels his praise is worthless. As Watzlawick says,

> He can casually discredit anybody who loves him, for there is evidently something wrong with a person who loves somebody who is unworthy of love. (Watzlawick, 1983, p43)

Similarly, when children who feel worthless meet with luck, or are given something nice, they may (outside of their conscious awareness) find a way of spoiling or 'losing' it, because deep down they feel they don't deserve it. After all, worthless people don't deserve good things.

Simon, aged fifteen

Fifteen-year-old Simon, who had been taken into care because his mother couldn't cope with him, spent two weeks decorating his room lovingly, and with great care. When it was finished, it looked beautiful. The care home gave him some new furniture to make it even nicer. Simon spent one night in his room, but in the morning started to tear down the wallpaper and destroy furniture, until his room looked bleak and broken. When asked why, he said that the wallpaper and new furniture were a lie. They presented too much of a contradiction between his inner feelings of being 'pathetic' (self-reference) and the outward reality of his bedroom as 'so lovely'.

Like Simon, many children who feel intrinsically bad or unworthy spoil goodness, or find a way of cutting it short, because they feel they do not deserve it. Similarly any achievements are often not enjoyed. 'It was just luck' is a common retort of the child with low self-esteem who has just done well in a test. The underlying belief is that if there is a 'success' around, it clearly isn't anything to do with me. A classic example is Tennessee Williams, the playwright, who became extremely successful, but it didn't fit in with his low self-esteem (a legacy from his painful childhood). As Berke states:

> The 'catastrophic success' of his play *The Glass Menagerie* snatched him from virtual oblivion and thrust him into a sudden prominence. In his new expensive Manhattan suite, things began to break 'accidentally'. Cigarettes would fall onto and damage the furniture. Windows would be left open in a downpour, and his room would be flooded – events that had never happened to him before. He became very depressed. (Berke, 1989, p153)

Some clever children with low self-worth are proud of what they achieve, and yet their achievements are never sufficient to change their image of themselves. Their sense of achievement can never be more than a veneer, offering moments of pleasure, but all too vulnerable to being smashed by the slightest criticism. In short, what a child achieves will ultimately do nothing to change their deeply ingrained sense of unloveability, although history is littered with people who have tried – for example, Marilyn Monroe, Tennessee Williams, Peter Sellers and Janis Joplin.

The child with low self-worth – prime target for both child and adult bullies

Many children who feel worthless put up with cruelty, unkindness or abuse of power far longer than someone with high self-regard. The latter will tend to have a far quicker and healthier response, and an attitude of 'I'm not putting up with this sort of treatment!' It takes self-esteem to speak out and say, 'Don't treat me like this!'; to say 'Stop', and 'I deserve better.' And if they need support from grown-ups to stop cruelty or unkindness happening, they will seek it out far more readily. The child who feels worthless may not seek out help from grown-ups, as deep down he may believe he deserves this bad treatment.

Children with very low self-esteem tend to attract persecutors. The child's hopelessness, passivity and feelings of worthlessness are picked up by the bullying child or adult, who can sense a victim. The child who feels worthless often exudes a feeling of 'I'm rubbish, so just treat me as such.' Sometimes, this is an irresistible invitation to people to do just that.

The bully's justification (usually outside of conscious awareness) is often that, 'She's giving a message to the world to kick her, so I will kick her. She is giving the message to the world that she is rubbish, so I will treat her as rubbish.' In response, the bullied child then has a gut response of, 'See. This is how the world is. It just proves I'm rubbish.' Effectively, the bullying other is doing to the child with low self-worth what he is doing to himself inside – inflicting cruelty. It is just that he is doing it to himself non-vocally with self-attack, self-criticism, and self-shaming, which continue to fuel his low self-worth on a daily basis.

The idealising of others, whilst unable to see the good in themselves

> That I should love a bright particular star
> And think to wed it, he is so above me.
> (Shakespeare, *All's Well That Ends Well*, I, 1, pp85–6)

Some children who feel worthless are often acutely and painfully aware of the perceived cleverness, popularity, good looks etc, they see in other children. These assets are often seen in an idealised, exaggerated way. Children who feel worthless can therefore move into a very split world: *all* good qualities are in others, and *all* the bad or inadequate ones are in themselves. A world seeming full of clever, popular, bright, sparky, good-looking people all around you, when you feel so worthless, can quickly become a persecutory world, in which the child suffers terribly. As Costello (1994, Personal Communication) explains: 'Whenever there is idealisation, there is denigration'.

The early and tragic life decision to be ordinary

Many people... may appear linguistically sterile, morally neutered, visually plain or depleted in energy. However, these are all camouflage, intended to deflect from what is actually interesting.... Sooner or later, when I have alertly hung around, the faded person will usually come out of hiding. For moments at least, he reveals something so arresting as to merit, like a character in a novel, even more widespread attention. In giving up the dulled image, such persons offer remarkably individualistic, suspenseful, and colourful memories, attitudes, expectations and insights. Having revealed these hoarded gems some will stay open and remain continuously interesting. Others will revert at the first sign of danger to the emptiness they have always banked on. (Polster, 1987, p4)

Some children with low self-worth may develop what Eric Berne describes as a 'banal life script' (1964, p108). This is an early decision (outside of conscious awareness) to lead an ordinary life, never to stand out from the crowd; to keep one's head down, and not to do anything extraordinary, or it's asking for trouble. The 'trouble' is anticipated shame, failure, exposure, and humiliation. The child projects on to the future what has been true for him in the past. This 'banal script' is a tragedy. As so eloquently put by psychotherapist Yalom, it is 'The refusal to become what he could [have] become' (Yalom, 1980, p282).

From low self-worth to a resigned complacency about their life and their lot

For some children, feeling worthless leads to a sense of resigned hopelessness and a feeling of inevitable failure: 'That's just how I am.' Experiencing failure, missed opportunities and disappointments becomes a way of life. They just don't fight for their corner. Some find a way to cut off so that they no longer feel the full pain of this. This defence is called hyper-inhibition or, more extremely, dissociation. (We will look at these defence mechanisms in the next part of the book.) Other children seem not to care any more, but this 'front' is just a disguise for the terrible, unspoken pain and grief they feel.

Low self-worth can have lifelong adverse effects on the ability to make it

Research has shown that feelings of low self-worth in childhood can affect performance in adulthood, far more than academic ability. Feinstein, at the Centre for Economic Performance, assessed data on children aged ten, collected through the 1970 British Cohort Study. He then looked at what these children were earning when in their twenties. The data showed that 'self-esteem at age ten was a very important indicator of high earnings in their twenties, far more than their academic ability when they were ten' (Feinstein, 2001, p20).

Living with the inner critic

> **Peter, aged fifteen**
> I am my own discourager, stopping only to take breath before delivering the next criticism, ... I try to run from myself but know I am my own pursuer. My pursuit of myself is without mercy.

The child with low self-esteem will inevitably live with an inner critic in his head. The inner critic is greatly responsible for his daily misery. The *inner critic* is largely composed of internalised verbal or non-verbal messages from people in his life such as parents, schoolteachers or bullies. These messages have been taken in and are now believed as the truth. Over time, they are often embellished and worsened by the child. He forgets their origin, that they were only opinions or primitive angry discharges from other people. He believes they are simply facts about who he is.

Sometimes this 'self-talk' develops into a kind of dialogue, referred to as the 'Nagger' and the 'Nagged at'.

The Nagger: 'You are so stupid. You can't draw, and everyone else in the class can.'
Nagged at: 'You are right, but I do try.'
The Nagger: 'Yes, but it's just not good enough.'

Inner bullying conversations such as these can take up too much of a child's emotional energy on a daily basis. Some inner critics are so relentless that they will blight the child's very spontaneity and creativity, stopping him from taking risks, stopping him from saying what he really wants to say. The critic is always there, with their relentless reminders of imminent failure, shame or humiliation. Children with particularly cruel self-critics can grow up without the confidence to follow any of their hopes and dreams.

It often takes counselling or therapy to bring into the child's conscious awareness this cruel discouraging 'sub-vocal dialogue' that is going on. Once in awareness the child can then be helped to deal with his inner critic (see exercise section).

From self-hate to self-sabotage

His self-hate was so intense that he took to hitting himself at night, a practice he resumed periodically even in adulthood. As a child he managed always to provoke punishment on his birthday and so be denied the planned celebration. (Bloch, 1978, p179)

Children who see themselves as 'too bad to feel good' often manufacture 'bad luck', which means that when anything good comes towards them, they unconsciously either side-step it or spoil it in some way. They lose their favourite toy, just miss being chosen to go on that special school trip because they put up their hand too late, or 'find' their best friend has gone off with someone else (in fact their best friend thinks they don't want to be *their* friend any more).

Tripping themselves up in these ways is not in the child's conscious awareness. It usually takes counselling or therapy for a child like this to see what he is doing, and to realise that his long run of 'bad luck' is not actually fate, but self-sabotage. Counselling or therapy can also help to prevent a life of 'bad luck'.

From self-hate to self-harm

> Most people treat themselves very badly, much worse than they would ever think of treating another human being. (Gendlin, 1978, p66)

Children with low self-worth can all too easily move into self-harm. For some children, this can be seen in the sheer numbers of their accidents – for example, bumping into things; accidently cutting themselves, and pushing their body beyond its limits. This can move into more terrible versions in adolescence – cutting themselves, standing on glass, swallowing drawing-pins – which are often far more distressing to the people around them than to the young people themselves. Many young people carry out these awful acts in a very cut-off, matter-of-fact way, albeit following an irresistible impulse to do so. Self-harm is all to easily habit-forming. There are many reasons why young people self-harm, but in each case, there is an underlying tortured relationship with the body-self. Furthermore, suffering can become a bizarre mode of self-soothing for the self-hating child; we shall see why in the next chapter.

From low self-esteem to eating disorders or distorted body image

> The poor duckling was terrified; just as he was trying to hide his head under his wing, a huge and frightful dog stood before him... showed his sharp teeth, and then – splash! He was off without touching the bird. 'Oh, thank goodness,' sighed the duckling. 'I'm so ugly that even the dog thinks twice before biting me.' (Andersen, 1994, pp102–3)

Self-hate can all too easily be transferred to the body: 'I hate myself because I am so ugly, fat, short, etc.'; 'I am unlovable because of the way I look.' Such body-hate can then lead to social phobias – for example, not wanting to be seen in any state of undress, or fear of public places in case people point or laugh at your body, which to you feels enormously conspicuous (whereas, of course, to others it is usually not even in their awareness).

Repeated attacking of the body with self-talk – 'You're so fat/slow/ugly/repulsive' – occurs particularly with young people in puberty and adolescence. Yet now surveys show that some girls of primary school age also obsess that their bottom might be too big, even if they are very skinny. Other children with tortured relationships with their body literally 'eat away at themselves', by biting nails down to the quick, or by repeatedly picking at spots until they bleed.

> I accidentally glanced into the mirror. My agitated face seemed utterly revolting: pale, spiteful, mean, my hair dishevelled. 'Well, I'm even quite pleased about that,' I thought. 'I'm really pleased that I shall appear revolting to her; it appeals to me...' (Dostoevsky, 1991, p84)

From low self-esteem to anti-social behaviour

> ☆ 'I am rubbish, so I may as well *be* rubbish.' (Tessa, aged eight)
>
> ☆ 'If I can't be good at making, at least I can be good at breaking.' (Simon, aged seven)

Of course, not all anti-social or bullying children have low self-esteem. Some children become anti-social because they had known too much unkindness and cruelty, or too many submission–dominance interactions. Yet these children may have a fairly robust self-esteem. This is because they have felt loved and delighted in by a parent for enough of the time. Picture, for example, the alcoholic father who is very proud of his four-year-old son, Tom, and shows this repeatedly. Yet when the father is drunk he shouts and hits Tom, and his wife. Tom in turn hits other children in the playground, and yet has no problem taking praise from his teacher for his writing or drawing. He knows his father loves him and is proud of him.

That said, some children's bad behaviour *is* motivated primarily by low self-esteem. These are children who no longer look for attention in the form of approval, because deep down they are certain that they won't get it. So they settle for attention in the form of disapproval – and this they find they can get easily. They believe that they can never bring anything good into the world, but that they can bring *something* into the world, even if it's bad. Eric Fromm, in his book *The Anatomy of Human Destructiveness* (1973), writes very eloquently about how an intrinsic part of the human condition is the need to make an impact. If a child cannot do this positively, he may try to do it negatively.

'If I feel bad about myself, I'll cope by making you feel bad.'

Some children attack other children verbally or physically as a way of dealing with what they themselves have suffered. It makes them feel big to make someone else feel small. (Several schools of psychotherapy also believe that passing on to others what has been done to oneself is a form of communication.) Such children usually do not have the self-awareness to know that they are simply handing on to others their own intolerable feelings of impotence, degradation, and shame. As Jung said, 'Everything unconscious is projected' (1982, p86).

Some children bolster their self-esteem by joining the bullying gang. They can feel they are 'someone' if they belong to such a group, as opposed to 'no-one' on their own. It is an escape into power.

The manic defence of 'I am worthless, so I will be famous'; 'I am nobody, so I will be somebody.'

Sometimes he would go to his room and there, in his own protected space, dream the dreams of glory that enabled him to repair a battered and undermined sense of himself. These dreams would materialize a world in which he could do anything... be acclaimed, and then triumphantly appear before his parents to show how wrong they had been in telling him so many times that he would be a nothing. He imagined laying his treasures at his mother's feet, wiping away her black moods and sullen withdrawals. Once and for all he would reclaim his heritage by restoring her world, which – he was forever being told with a thousand cues, raised eyebrows, and turned-down corners of a mouth – had collapsed because of something he had done or failed to do. (Stolorow et al, 1987, p60)

The blighted child can be very different in his imagination. He can escape the pain of shame and humiliation, as Superman in one form or another. For some children who feel worthless, this escape into imagination becomes a rehearsal of the possible. They become total workaholics, giving up a childhood of fun in the attempt to be top or first in some prized school subject. Many people in showbiz started off like this and moved into a 'I'll show them' that bore fruit. The trouble is that usually, despite their outer success, the worthless impotent child lives on to haunt them. This renders their success meaningless, 'Just luck' or 'They are just not seeing the real me.'

Some children who feel worthless, deeply ordinary or unspecial grow up with a burning need to be special or famous in the eyes of the world. In other words, they look to the world to find the benign, encouraging, admiring mirror they failed to find in the significant adults in their lives. Freud called it a reaction formation – for example, to move from 'I'm awful, hate me', to 'I'm wonderful, love me' (1979, p157). For many people, this comes crashing down at some time in later life. As Alice Miller states, 'That balloon flew up very high in a good wind but then suddenly got a hole and soon lay like a little rag on the ground. For nothing genuine that could have strength and support later on had ever developed' (1987, p57).

A summary of common ways children deal with their feelings of worthlessness or self-hate

• *Project their feelings on to other children (through bullying)*	Make other children feel bad, useless, incompetent; in other words, whatever they feel about themselves.
• *Transfer their feelings of self-hate on to their body*	Displace their feelings on to their body and so suffer a tortured relationship with their body – eating disorders, self-mutilation, minor 'accidents'. The ugly, unacceptable body may be easier to bear than the feeling of the unacceptable self.
• *Anaesthetise their feelings*	Numb themselves against the painful feelings of self-criticism and self-hate, leaving them feeling emotionally flat, dull, and empty. We know from neuroscience that it is indeed possible to numb oneself emotionally against too painful feelings.
• *Drown out their feelings*	More a phenomenon in adolescents with feelings of low self-worth who move into drink, drugs, sleeping too much.
• *Try to beat them by a manic defence of 'I'll show them I am important, or special!'*	The problem is that this child manically defending against feelings of worthlessness by trying to be excellent, superb, very good-looking etc., can become totally driven. He may miss out on his childhood by being obsessed with maths, or playing the piano, etc; trying to be the best, because underneath he feels so worthless. Often, for such children, mistakes are terrible. By building up such a successful or perfect persona these children then totally deprive themselves of feeling loved for who they really are – warts and all.

UNDERSTANDING A CHILD'S FEELINGS OF WORTHLESSNESS

Why a deep, loving human connection in early life is at the very core of self-esteem

> The mother... reveals by the light and expression on her face the nature of the baby in her mind which is there to be read by the baby and which forms the basis for his developing self-image from the beginning of life outside the womb. (Reid, 1990, p48)

A deep, loving connection to someone in childhood is a vital foundation if a child is to develop positive self-esteem. This connection is not necessarily to a parent; it may be to a nanny, auntie or grandparent. But it has to be a person who is around enough of the time, otherwise a connection cannot deepen and develop. Only relationships that have been nurtured over time can profoundly influence the emotion biochemistry in the child's brain which, as we shall see, is a core factor for self-esteem.

A deep connection to someone is not equivalent to having felt loved by someone. A child may have felt loved by a parent with whom he had a somewhat weak or ambivalent connection.

A deep connection is a relationship in which

✫ The child consistently feels appreciated, encouraged, and very known for who he is in a totally non-judgmental way.

✫ The child feels soothed and calmed when distressed.

✫ The child feels accepted for who he is, not for the other person's version of who he is – or who they want him to be.

✫ The child doesn't have to hide any of his feelings to feel accepted – for example, grief, anger, fear, anxiety, passion, love. In other words, there is something big enough and strong enough in this other person to be undaunted by the child's intense emotions. As Thomas Moore says, 'The word intimacy means "profoundly interior"… In our intimate relationships, the "most within" dimensions of ourselves and the other are engaged' (Moore, 1992, p212).

☆ When the child is at his most fully alive, fully rejoicing, fully grieving, fully angry, etc, the other person will respond without closing off, without persuading him out of the feeling he is having, or becoming judgmental.

☆ With this other person, the child feels safe enough to:
  – Play
  – Laugh
  – Get excited
  – Be spontaneous
  – Cry
  – Get angry
  – Tell their deepest secrets
  – Tell their deepest pain

☆ The child knows this person will take the time to understand fully what he is feeling, and to check with him that he has got it right.

☆ The child knows that he will be remembered by this person in his absence. It is terribly important to children to know they live in the mind of their loved one, rather than 'fall out of it' when they are not there. As one six-year-old boy said to his therapist, 'Will you forget me when I'm gone? I'm afraid you will.'

☆ The child knows that with this person, their imagination, thoughts and feelings may all be actively engaged in some way.

☆ The two should bring out something very alive in each other. As Hycner says, 'There is a meeting of something deep inside of me with something deep inside this other person' (1993, p7).

☆ With this other person, the child experiences the feeling of 'thriving' and of being very alive.

In short, with this person the child visits some of the richest vistas of human relating possible. Being together with this other person takes the child into truly creative ways of being – into a whole array of colours, tones, and hues of shared emotional energy states: calm, bubbly, excited, loving, tender, quiet, passionate, fascinated. It brings him the deepest sense of being valued. It is all this that can enable the child to weather so well many of life's trials, to maintain a strong sense of hope in the face of adversity, and a certainty about the goodness and beauty in the world.

With a deep connection such as this, firmly established in childhood, the child's adult life may of course be very painful at times – nothing can save him from that – but the pain is far less likely to send him plummeting into despair and hopelessness. Similarly, if people do shame, bully, discourage or criticise him, they will not destroy his self-esteem. Furthermore, if the criticism is given by someone bearing him goodwill, he will not feel attacked, but will take it on board as potentially useful feedback. He may decide to change something about his feeling, thinking or behaving as a result. If, however, the criticism is given by someone who does not bear him good will (for example, given out of envy, hate, or malice) then he may indeed go into a place of shame or doubt – but only temporarily, before he re-connects with his fundamental deep-down belief in his basic worth as a human being.

Some important quotations from psychotherapy about the power of deep connection in the establishing of both self-esteem and love of life

> ...one part of ourselves that we cherish is the wealth we have accumulated through our relations to people, for these relations and also the emotions that are bound up with them have become an inner possession. (Klein, 1988, p340)

> A soul mate is someone to whom we feel profoundly connected, as though the communicating and communing that takes place between us were not the product of intentional efforts, but rather a divine grace. This kind of relationship is so important to the soul that many have said there is nothing more precious in life. (Moore, 1994, pxviii)

> All real living is meeting. (Buber, 1958, p11)

> Connection with another always both actualises and expands the self... (Mitchell, 1995, p277)

> This process of displacing love [from a person to a love of life] is of the greatest importance for the development of the personality and of human relationships; indeed, one may say, for the development of culture and civilisation as a whole. (Klein, 1946)

Low self-worth – because the connection between parent and child went wrong

> Sally and Mike [parents]... didn't know that babies and little kids need to laugh, and be held... and be warm and fed... and be smiled at... and tickled. (Hughes, 1998, p121)

In this quotation, Hughes makes a vital point. Some parents never experienced a deep connection (as described above) with someone in *their own* childhood, so as a result, they may not know how to connect in this way with *their* child. As Oscar Wilde said, 'We all need love, but who can do the loving?' Yet for a child, not to feel very very special to someone by whom they feel deeply known, means that the vital foundation to their self-esteem cannot be laid down.

Being unsure as to whether they are special to their parent – unsure if they are held very dear in heart and mind – is the fate of some children. They have never felt themselves to be their parent's prince or princess – a birthright for every child.

Samantha, aged thirteen

Samantha, had made three suicide attempts. Her parents had given her up for adoption at two. When seeing the psychiatrist she said, 'I was a good baby. Why wasn't I special to them?' This wound of feeling unloved, unknown and unappreciated by the person you desperately need to love you, know you and appreciate you, can lead to a state of deep despair. Children do not understand this as being due to their parents' problems with loving. They so often see it as their own fundamental 'unloveability'.

Eddie, aged twelve

Eddie was living in care. He kept spiders. Eddie's self-esteem was at rock bottom, due to being rejected by the most important person in his life – his mother. Eddie loved his spiders and would kiss them and make little beds for them, but when he felt bad about himself the spiders all mysteriously died. Then one day, Eddie tried to kill himself. That is what can happen to a little boy when he is rejected by the most important person in his life. Luckily, Eddie was given a therapist. With her help, he was able to understand how the spiders represented his vulnerable infant self, which had felt so 'killed off' by his mother's rejection. He had needed help to begin to grieve. Therapy provided him with that help.

The small child loses self-esteem when he loses love and attains it when he regains love...children...need...[ongoing, mirroring] supplies of affection...' (Fenichel, 1945, p41)

When a parent doesn't bond with her child – the effect on self-esteem

Hephaestus, the Smith-god, was so weakly at his birth that his disgusted mother, Hera, dropped him from the height of Olympus, to rid herself of the embarrassment that his pitiful appearance caused her... (Graves, 1964, pp86–7)

Winnicott (a psychoanalyst) describes how most mothers will naturally bond with their baby. He calls this 'primary maternal preoccupation' (1965). But some mothers are too depressed, too distressed, too exhausted, too drained, too under-supported or too full of their own anxieties to be able to form a close bond with their baby.

We know from neurobiological research that if a mother is clinically depressed or in a state of high distress, anxiety or rage, then too high levels of the stress chemicals – noradrenaline and adrenaline – and too high levels of the stress hormone – cortisol – can block her maternal chemicals (opioids and oxytocin). This is a psychobiochemical reality. She is not a bad parent. This is just how things are.

Sometimes the mother's distress in parenting is caused by the triggering of painful feelings about her own infancy, because she in turn had a parent who could not cope with *her* helplessness, neediness and demands when *she* was a baby. Because of this, she may find the helplessness of her own baby abhorrent. Unless she has been in psychotherapy, she is unlikely to appreciate why she is feeling as she does.

Some mothers have real problems with the needy, totally dependent part of their babies, because it triggers off their own unmet infantile needs. The baby's intense feelings may sometimes therefore be too close to the ones the mother experiences, but which she is trying to suppress or forget.

Another parent may be loving when her baby is being sweet and affectionate, yet turn away or become angry when he is in an extreme state of unhappiness or anger. In other words, she may only be able to love an idealised version of her baby, not her real baby. This again may be because her own 'primitive' baby self was never met with compassion and soothing by *her* parents.

For whatever reason, this tormented start in life can lead the infant to a profound sense of being unwanted, rejected and fundamentally undesirable. It is not hard to see how the child with low self-worth has internalised these responses, seeing himself as without value, or worse, as a person worthy of the hate or disgust of others.

The Home Office statistics on the murder of infants tell us that: 'The biggest group of people in this country who are murdered are all under the age of one year old' (Home Office, 1994, pp71–4). This shows just how tormented some mothers are by the feelings provoked in them by their baby. This tragedy of infanticide does not speak of all the children who are not actually physically harmed, and yet who nevertheless feel the hate and raging impulses of their parents.

'I cannot light my Mummy up... There must be something wrong with me'

A deeper and even more dreadful experience – the experience of the faceless mother, that is, the mother whose face does not light up at the sight of her child. (Kohut, 1984, p21) (See Figure 1)

Some infants simply fail to light up their parent. Too often they meet with tepid or disinterested responses, or indifference. The little things they do – approaches, smiles, pointings-to, small love gifts – feel like they count for too little. Too many of his parent's facial expressions show the child that he is *not* the apple of her eye. Too infrequently does the parent get down on the floor and play dolls, or cars or castles with him. Too infrequently does she scoop him up in her arms and cuddle him with delight. These are not 'bad' or unkind parents, they are often parents who simply do not know how to relate to a baby or toddler, as no-one related well to or played well with *them* when *they* were a child.

A child who fails too often to light up his parent is likely to learn some tragic lessons very early in life. These lessons can then be generalised to other important relationships. Some of the tragic lessons are that:

Figure 1 The faceless mother

'Through her use of her mother as a mirror, Katie (age 2) could only conclude that she herself was worthless and of no special interest or value. She would further conclude that [her mother] held little pleasure or joy for her. Her mother would gradually become an object to manipulate in order to get things or to attack when she became the source of discomfort.' (Hughes, 1998, p21)

✬ Whatever he does, he cannot elicit states of joy in the other.

✬ His loving feelings are not of value.

✬ There must be something wrong with him, or inadequate about him to elicit such indifferent reactions.

✬ He must be basically unlovable; otherwise, he reasons, of course his parent would delight in him.

In certain tests, mothers were asked to look at their babies for a while with a blank face (Murray, 1988, p159). Videos detailing the second-by-second interaction between the blank-faced mother and child show how, when the mother's loving gaze was not forthcoming, the baby tried hard to get her to look at him. It was found that the babies then became disturbed by this. They tried at first to protest, and then withdrew and looked away from their mother's face, or made short, darting glances to her. After a while, the baby disengages completely. In real life, if this happens time after time, the baby can appear lifeless and lethargic.

Dead-to-me

And when we are together for some little time,
We share the room with many deaths.
Your unfired eyes which find no interest here,
Your body set in restless frame,
Already with the next thing.
Always with the next thing.
And you'll mistake my swallowed cries,
Neatly tidied behind a mouth of please-you-smile,
For contented child face.

Margot Sunderland

Infants with 'faceless' mothers (often because the mother is depressed) become passive and withdrawn. Their state of low arousal – bodily and emotionally – can extend to their school lives, and sometimes into adulthood. In short, these children have not been naturally lit up with a love of life. Henry Massie, an American psychotherapist, completed a 30-year study showing how early deadened mother–infant interactions can still affect people in adulthood. His research was fully backed up by video footage of mother with baby, and then again at various times throughout the adult's life, culminating in an adult interview. In one particular case, a mother robotically spooned food into her baby's mouth with no words or interaction. At 30, the man was still complaining of lifelessness, problems in relationships, and not having enough energy to complete things (Massie, 2003).

How different this is from the picture of the mother and child besotted with each other, where each delighted interaction lays down another vital foundation stone of high self-esteem. Enid Balint (psychoanalyst) describes such a joyous union beautifully: 'The eager aliveness in two people, the infant with the potential for life and the mother alive inside herself and tuning in to the emerging infant' (Balint, 1993, p102).

The vital connection between a child's self-esteem and the 'world of the face'

The mother, then, reveals by the light and expression on her face, the nature of the baby in her mind, which is there to be read by the baby and which forms the basis for his developing self-image from the beginning of life. (Reid, 1990, p48)

If a child meets light in the face of his parent figure at the age of about two months, he starts to engage in long, loving eye contact. As Stern says, 'It is an exquisitely interpersonal time, a time before he is able to talk, walk, explore. He has entered "a face world"' (1990, p60).

This period of 'face world' lasts between two and six months. If the infant misses out on it, then something very special has been lost, that for some people may never come again in such an intense way. And what is lost with it, are vital foundation stones for self-esteem. The following are statements from children whose mothers were post-natally depressed, and who therefore could not offer their babies this lovely face world.

Figure 2 The foundation stones of high self-esteem are located in babyhood not childhood

'He and his caregiver have no specific subject matter...Their only topic is the single moment, happening now, two human beings mutually engaged. These interactions' only goal is to sustain that experience. They are not preliminary to something else; they are that something.' (Stern, 1990, p51)

'The infant needs to be able to discover his/her capacity to light up the mother's face – for here is to be found the fundamental basis of self-esteem.' (Casement, 1990, p93)

Toby, aged six

At the beginning of counselling, Toby said, 'I'm rubbish. I've always known it.' Toby had never been able to light up his mother, who had suffered from severe post-natal depression. She said she had never really bonded with him after that.

Angela, aged four
When Angela was born, her mother was grieving the death of *her* own mother. Her heart was with her dead mother, and not with baby Angela. When Angela was four, her mother said to her in a fit of rage that she did not want her.

Angela's story: 'There was nothing the tortoise could do but die.' Everything was either dead or drowning in Angela's stories.

Moreover, the power of this early face-to-face interaction in terms of self-esteem is deeply grounded in neurobiological evidence. When the child engages in delightful interactions with his parent – laughing together, peek-a-boo games, conversations of sounds and gestures – there are all manner of positive arousal chemical firings in his brain: cascades of dopamine, serotonin, oxytocin and endorphins, for example. When we engage with people in harsh, dull or deadened ways, these lovely chemical cascades do not happen. In fact, excessive levels of stress chemicals can be released instead.

Dopamine and opioids are regularly activated in a child's brain by delightful parent–infant interactions. The activation of these chemicals in the brain is essential for positive arousal states such as hope, optimism, determination, and happiness – the very states lacked by so many children with low self-esteem. Dopamine is also vital for curiosity, interest in learning, and the wish to explore. The activation of dopamine in the brain is essential for a child to enjoy 'an energised state of engagement in the world' (Panksepp, 1998, p150). So much so, that when dopamine is firing too weakly in the brain, then it can be very difficult to feel interested in anything. Desire just isn't strong enough… for anything. As Panksepp says: 'Without dopamine, human aspirations remain frozen, as it were, in an endless winter of discontent' (1998, p144).

In infancy, essential dopaminergic systems are still being established in the brain. They are not finished at birth. This makes the lovely shared times between parent and child even more important. In fact lovely interactions regulate the growth and development of the dopaminergic cells in the higher brain, and enhance brain development as a whole. Strong activation of dopamine in a child's brain in the first years of his life also affects the genes that influence the flow of opioids (lovely calming chemicals in the brain). As Damasio says, 'There are biological mechanisms behind the most sublime human behaviour' (1996, p183).

Some neuroscientists believe that if an infant misses this special developmental phase of positive face world, he is danger of establishing a habitual chemical balance with lower levels of these positive arousal brain chemicals, making him vulnerable to low self-esteem and depression in later life. And yet all too often parents do not realise just how powerful these joyous interactions are for the child's self-esteem and for his developing emotional brain. So much so that statistics show that in the UK on average children watch television 28 hours a week, and have in comparison only 40 minutes time in conversation with their parents.

> As far back as he could remember it seemed his parents would avert their eyes from his when speaking with him. How lonely and anxious he felt at those times – as if he were not there. (Rowe & MacIsaac, 1989, p46)

When children feel their love is of little value – the effects on self-esteem

> The experiences of falling in love and being in love have a rich early developmental story. (Stern, 1990, p180)

An infant's first love gifts for his mother – a smile or, later, a little cluster of daisies – are not little things: rather, they are charged with meaning. Take, for example, a two-year-old boy who finds a leaf on the pavement and gives it as a love gift to his mother. He presents it to her with a look of delighted expectation. If his gift is received well, he becomes more enlivened and energised. The moment is made richer because it has become a shared moment. His joy builds and builds as he sees her face and hears her voice responding to him in a delighted way. The world then seems to him to be a beautiful place.

But if his mother doesn't respond well – brushes him aside, or tells him not to bother her now – he can feel a deep sense of shame and rejection. His world can seem to fall apart. If his smiles, spontaneous hugs and early love gifts of 'bits of fluff from the carpet' are worth so little to Mummy, there can be a feeling that, 'I have nothing good to bring to Mummy, and so there is nothing good in me.'

Figure 3

'We may choose to grow, to stagnate or to decline, and in a world where there is little encouragement to grow, most of us may not do it very much at all.' (Rowan, 1986, p13)

If his approaches, loving glances, touches, cuddles or smiles repeatedly fail to engage his parent, he can feel so deeply discouraged that his spontaneity, expressiveness, aliveness and desire to engage others is markedly diminished. His approach behaviour will be blighted, as it is too linked to associations with shame. As Kohut says, '[The parent] fails to respond with... pride or with other appropriate reactions that the child needs in order to maintain his self-esteem... Moreover, this parental failure comes at a moment when the child's self... is only precariously established and thus especially vulnerable' (1984, p32).

As the next poem suggests, experiencing indifference or rejection from the person you desperately want and need to love you, may not only have devastating effects on a child's self-esteem, but may also harden his heart. Loving has brought just too much pain. He may not dare to love again.

Rupture

Her rushing away
Snaps him off her,
Like the breaking of a candy-stick
Quick, that quick, she who made him
The brittle blowing in their faces,
And before she leaves, she dangles
His love, and drops it in a little bin.
Then tragedy crashes into him,
And he's capsized in the storms of his own yearning,
Uglied from both terrible shock
And complete knowing, that she always goes
Because she does not want to stay.
But as his body moves yet still,
She does not see the little death
The curse on all forgotten ones
Who go on breathing, yet are dead.
And so she lets him come to her
In the dusk of her still warm from another's touch;
His coming like a leaded drone
His eyes too full of faraway.

Margot Sunderland

When early infantile shaming resulting from 'blind' or insensitive parental response has assaulted a child, its consequences can run amok in later life. He may be left with a feeling that there must be something terribly wrong with him; that he is too greedy, or too needy, or too undesirable. He may be left with no sense of his essential goodness. As Fairbairn explains in this most important passage, the infant whose love is unreciprocated may end up 'exploding ineffectively' (1952b, p113).

His... love of his mother, in the face of rejection at her hands... is equivalent to discharging his love into an emotional vacuum. Such a discharge is accompanied by an [emotional] experience which is singularly devastating. In the older child this experience is one of intense humiliation over the depreciation of his love, which seems to be involved. At a somewhat deeper level (or at an earlier stage) the experience is one of shame over the display of needs that are disregarded or belittled. By virtue of these experiences of humiliation and shame [the baby] feels reduced to a state of worthlessness, destitution or beggardom. His sense of his own value is threatened: and he feels bad in the sense of 'inferior'. At a still deeper level (or at a still earlier stage) the child's experience is one of, so to speak, exploding ineffectively... It is thus an experience of disintegration and of imminent psychical death. (Fairbairn, 1952b, p113)

Figure 4 Without the meeting of essential relational needs within an attachment relationship, a child cannot experience herself as being special and worthwhile

Toby, aged seven

Toby's mother said she had never really bonded with him. She felt very bad about it, but was at a loss as to how to 'make myself love him more'.

In play therapy, Toby made up stories: 'The baby frog looks for the Mummy frog, but he never reaches her. Something has happened to the baby frog's heart. It has made the ice age come. Even tears get frozen.'

Week after week in play therapy, the baby frog kept failing to reach Mummy frog. On one occasion, the baby frog was thrown out of the plane on the way to see the Mummy. On another, the bus crashed. The therapist said, 'It seems so hard for the Mummy frog and the baby frog to come together.' Toby became very pensive. Then he said, 'You know, the frog is so hungry. He has been since he was a baby.' In another session Toby said, 'The frog is getting younger and younger and now he's a baby.' He then put the little frog next to the Mummy frog and said, 'I think they should start again, right from the beginning.' He then sat on the therapist's lap and put his head on her shoulder. As the therapy developed, Toby started to see how lovely he was in the eyes of his therapist. His school work improved, he started to make friends and his school reported that he was much much happier. Through his relationship with his therapist, Toby found his first love. He found a grown-up he could light up, a grown-up whom he knew would gently take him in her mind and keep him 'in mind' even when she wasn't there!

Born in Mind

Nestled
On a lull of time
Among your contemplative dreams,
A weightless stretch of whispered calm
Your voice a wash of cradling sound.
And so unveiled this world of ease
That sings its glow of thrill and light,
From here in you I drink it in,
There is such lovely here.

Margot Sunderland

> **Gemma, aged eight**
>
> Gemma's mother had lost her husband just after Gemma was born. Her relationship with her daughter had been damaged as a result. This was Gemma's story in play therapy:
>
> 'There's this moon and this cat. The cat jumps over the moon in case the moon gets angry. But really the cat would just like to snuggle into the moon and curl up and go to sleep.'

Parental depression – some common effects on a child's self-esteem

[He] did not feel enticing enough to draw [her] out of her depression. (Solomon, 1985, p62)

Some depressed parents are excellent with their children. Their depression does not stop them conversing in an enlivened way. For some depressed parents, their child is what makes them want to keep going. So we are talking here only of a depression that severely interrupts the bonding between mother and child. As we have seen, in clinical depression the release of brain chemicals that engender maternal feelings is blocked by excessive levels of stress chemicals and hormones. As a result, during this time the good connection between mother and child is lost.

A clinically depressed parent can be:

✰ Too defeated about life to 'bring to life' her child.

✰ Too anxious and overwhelmed, so the child cannot 'feel felt' by her.

✰ Too 'full of her own feelings', so she is 'mind-blind' (Siegel, 1999, p105) to the feelings of her child.

For some mothers, the mental anguish of post-natal depression brings all manner of torment to both themselves and their child. The child's crying, neediness or incessant demands can activate hate or murderous feelings in her (again a psychobiological reality where too high levels of cortisol block the brain's positive arousal chemicals).

A parent who is clinically depressed, or emotionally unavailable, can of course feel all the pain and guilt and torment of not being able to give to her child the loving responsiveness she knows he so badly needs. She may be all too painfully aware that she cannot find enough 'desire' in herself to play with her child, talk to him, cuddle him, gaze at him with interest and delight, tell him stories, sing to him, stay close while he falls asleep, or let him fall asleep in her arms. She may be painfully aware that too often she feels like withdrawing from him, instead of approaching him with delight. Of course the child takes all this personally. Of course, he doesn't understand about clinical depression and how at a fundamentally neurological level it blocks the loving chemicals in his mother's brain. He doesn't understand therefore, that her harsh or indifferent responses have nothing whatsoever to do with his assumed unlovability. Tragically, some children will desperately try to delight, amuse and bring back to life their depressed mother, but to no avail. 'It's all my fault that I cannot make my Mummy happy.' said Sally, aged seven.

Research shows that infants' brains can be affected by depression in their mothers – the neurological basis to the infant's unhappiness:

> Researchers at the University of Washington ... compared frontal-lobe EEG measures in the infants of depressed and non-depressed mothers. By about one year of age, babies whose mothers are depressed do indeed exhibit a different pattern of neural responsiveness than control babies. During playful interactions, like a game of peekaboo, they experience less activation of the left hemisphere [the 'feel-good' side of the brain] than control babies. (Eliot, 1999, p47)

However, with a parent whose depression is a mood, not an illness, she can be exhausted, irritable or extremely frustrated, but the child still feels that he can find a loving connection with her, because she still smiles at him, or holds him very close to her in a loving way, and her voice is still warm when she talks to him. Of course, there may be times when she loses all of this, when the child feels he's lost his good connection with her, but then she sees the pain and fear in his face, and so takes the time to mend things between them. Or she hands him over to someone else he knows well, until she can reconnect with the warmth in herself.

The danger comes when a mother does not realise that the child has moved into anguish because he feels he's lost his good connection with her, and so she does not mend the connection between them. She does not take the time to hold him close and lovingly until he is 'put back together again'.

From too many weak or shallow connections with a parent-figure to low self-esteem

> At 32 I went into therapy because I just couldn't tell my son that I loved him. (Mother of a six-year-old boy.)

Some parents don't really know how to establish a deep connection with their child. It is not that they do not or cannot love, it is simply that they find it difficult to express this to their child . They find it difficult to interact with their child in ways that deepen their relationship. The problem then is that despite the child being loved, he may grow up not feeling loved, and so cannot love himself.

A child may grow up with low self-worth, because the emotional connection between him and his parent/s was never strong enough. It was too weak to enliven him and to enable him to experience human relationship as a source of joy, pleasure or comfort. It has left him with just too little actual experience of the potential of relationship; of relationship as being enriching and profoundly satisfying. Instead, he has had too much experience of relationship as something dull or deadening. Without positive powerful connections with a parent-figure at the start of life, it can be really difficult for a child to develop his self-esteem into something solid and secure.

Examples of weak emotional connections between parents/children

☆ Being somewhat reserved, polite or formal, on both sides.

☆ Misconnections – where a child's expressions of what he is feeling are not met, or are misinterpreted. For example, 'You're just tired dear.'

☆ The child sells out to total compliance and being too good, so as not to rock the boat.

☆ The parent's own disillusionment with intimacy and relationship is passed on to the child.

☆ The child encounters something too lifeless or defeated in the parent.

The parent is not comfortable with spontaneous hugs and touches, or with rough-and-tumble play.

> The quality of contact determines whether life 'passes by' or whether it is lived and experienced to the full. (Clarkson, 1989, p34)

Ben, aged twelve

Ben was offered therapy at his school, because he seemed so emotionally flat a lot of the time. He had also worried the teacher by once describing himself as feeling like 'just a brain on legs'. Ben was brought up in a family where all connections were rather formal. Ben was a very good boy, and would always do what his parents asked of him. Both parents were uncomfortable with physical contact, as were their parents before them. In therapy, Ben reported being bored whenever he went out with his parents. He also remembered playing on his own a lot. He said, 'Why would anyone want to live with someone? I get far more out of being with my computer than I do being with people.' Although Ben enjoyed hours of pleasure from his computer, he told the therapist that he often thought life was a rather dull affair.

'Look, Mummy – isn't it amazing!': The importance of adults acknowledging excited states

> Certain kinds of interpersonal experiences are necessary for the growth of the self; when these are lacking, central features of the child remain buried, unevoked, frozen. (Mitchell, 1988, p161)

One of the stages of child development from the age of about 18 months to three years, is defined by the psychologist Eric Erickson as 'Autonomy versus Shame and Doubt' (1977, p243). This is a stage at which a child can start to feel very proud of something he can do, or express. It is very common for children at this crucial stage to express great pride in what they are doing – 'Mummy, look what I did!'; 'Mummy look at me!' (coming down the big slide); 'What a big noise I can make, a big jump I can do!' If in his moment of pride, the child is met with an encouraging, appreciative response from a parent or teacher, he will start to build up a sense of his own potency, and go on to trust his creativity and spontaneity. He will build a strong sense of 'I am someone who can make things happen, and what I make happen can be good and worthwhile.' Sometimes a child can feel as though the delighted response of his mother to his own squeals of delight is as if they are 'flying together', metaphorically speaking. It's an exhilarating experience.

In contrast, where over time a child meets with too many negative responses or flat non-responses to his spontaneous joyous outbursts, he is likely to grow up feeling wary, defeated or shameful in terms of who he is and what he can do. He may start to hold back. He may lose his spontaneity, as it is too linked in his mind to shame. Persistently busy, preoccupied parents may just too often give the message 'Not now dear, we're dealing with something far more important' (than the windmill/colour of your lollipop, spider on the path etc.) The child will feel belittled by this and learns that what he has to say counts for too little. The children's book *Not Now Bernard* illustrates this well. Bernard is telling his mother that there is a monster around. She keeps saying 'Not now, Bernard.' Eventually the monster eats Bernard and takes his place in Bernard's bed – and his parents don't even notice.

Timmy, aged five
When Timmy was five he painted a picture of an underwater world. He spent ages getting the bottom of the sea to look right, and the octopus's tentacles to wiggle in the right direction. When he had finished, he felt so very proud of it. In fact Timmy thought it was the best picture he had ever done. He showed it to his mother. It was a love gift for her. 'Look Mummy, look! It is for you.', he said with joy in his face. 'But submarines have funnels, now put them in like this.', replied his mother. Timmy's face registered a terrible blow. He had wanted so much more from her. If children like Timmy repeatedly meet with such killing responses to their creativity and spontaneity, the blight can run very deep. 'I am no good, and what I do is no good.' Or, 'I am of little worth and what I create is of little worth.'

Feeling loved for what you do, not for who you are

There was once a donkey who had worked very hard all his long life, but who at last grew old and weak. 'We must buy a strong new donkey,' said the peasant to his wife, 'and get rid of this useless old one.' (Barber, 1992, p34)

Some children suffer from low self-esteem because they never sense that simply being who they are is enough to make them lovable. Love always seems to have conditions attached. Self-worth may, for example, be based on the belief that 'I am loved only in so far as I am useful' – for example, '… if I look after my siblings.' or 'If I am Mummy's little helper.' Or 'I am loved only if I succeed.' When they fail a test at school, love in their parent turns to anger or cold withdrawal. This response can then all too easily be internalised, so if they are ever less than perfect, they start to give themselves a really hard time about it, with lots of attacking 'self-talk', such as 'You're so stupid for doing that/saying that.'

A child who only feels loved when he is perfect and doesn't make mistakes can all too easily learn to view his imperfections as deeply shameful, or unforgivable. This child can then feel driven to achieve and be successful at school. And if he fails in this, it can lead to more self-criticism and self-hate as he continues to battle in vain for love that often seems so far out of his reach. Demanding perfection from oneself automatically creates ever greater potential for failing to live up to one's ideals; and thus a far greater potential for self-blame. For children whose self-esteem is precariously balanced on the act of perfection or opportunities to excel, life is a driven affair, devoid of the knowledge essential for high self-esteem: 'Whatever you do or fail to do, this does not affect how much I as your parent love you.'

Feeling loved only if you have nice feelings

We quickly learned that those feelings and impulses were unlovable, and it was a short step to come to believe they were bad. It is easy to understand how we then lost touch with our deepest nature. If I have been taught that to be loveable I must harbour only good feelings… and if I have become convinced that my true self is full of bad feelings then I will set about trying to disavow the parts of me about which I have such gloomy suspicions. (Kahn, 1991, p45)

Some children develop a well-behaved and compliant façade to avoid disapproval. They will become whatever and whoever their parents need them to be. And with some parents, this means no less than total compliance. The child must be polite, well-behaved, tidy, smiling and helpful – all the time. Such a child will learn that to express intense feelings and needs is far too dangerous, as it will risk him losing his mother's love. In adulthood, such a child may continue to be nice and good all the time, as if he is consciously or unconsciously 'continually wanting to appease fantasised persecutors' (Rosenfeld, 1965, p101).

Ben, aged three

Every time Ben tried to cling to his mother, she called him 'weak' and a 'baby'. As Ben got older he believed that any needs he had were 'pathetic' and unacceptable. So he stopped going to his parents for comfort. When he was afraid, it didn't even occur to him to ask for help. Ben grew up as a fiercely independent, very well-behaved little boy. But at school he hated the children who cried for their mothers. He saw them as 'cry babies'. He attacked their perfectly natural, perfectly healthy feelings just as his own had been attacked.

Children quickly learn to adapt to their parents' view of what is loveable or 'good', even if it goes against who they are and what they feel. For many children, their intense need for their parent's approval means that it is simply not an option not to conform. But this is a rocky self-esteem indeed, based on an emotionally stifled version of oneself. As Johnson says, 'My life threatens my life. So, what is ultimately blocked is life force itself' (1994, p89).

> Metaphorically, we all wear an 'I want you to like me' sticker on our foreheads. Whether we are conscious of it or not (and most of us are not) much of our behaviour – good or bad – is simply part of an *act* that we developed as children in the hope that it would earn us much needed attention and/or approval. (Jeffers, 1992, p23)

The blight of shame and its toxic effect on self-esteem

> Shame accompanied Katie along her path. Shame permeated her sense of self... Shame is not a warm companion... Shame etches its message into her muscles, her heart, her mind: You are flawed. You bring no joy to others. You are bad and without merit. It screams: 'Yes I have no worth. I am worthless...' (Hughes, 1998, p23)

Shame is far more lethal than guilt. In guilt it is the act that is found bad; in shame, it is the actual self. Because of this, shaming can have profoundly damaging long-term effects on a child's self-esteem. When shamed a child will often feel absolutely awful about himself without knowing why. Shame impoverishes life, through inducing fear and self-doubt.

What shame does to a child's mind, body and feeling of self-worth

✪ It can make him feel worthless.

✪ It moves from the specific to the general, and so it can make the child paranoid that *everyone* is judging him negatively (often they are doing nothing of the sort).

✪ It can make the child hypersensitive to and hypervigilant for disapproval in the voice and face of others. '*She often feels watched – senses eyes on her, even when no-one is there*' (Blume, 1990, p49). Hence shame can move a child into a social phobia.

✪ A deeply shamed child will often avoid eye contact or look away, as he expects to see contempt or disapproval in the eyes of the other.

✪ It can make him feel totally devoid of all goodness and value.

✪ It makes the child want to withdraw, hide, avoid – an impulse that is often acted on. Neurobiologists call it a state of 'conservation-withdrawal'.

✪ It can make him feel ashamed to exist at all.

✪ It can make him feel that the whole of him is not-OK – not just his behaviour, but his very being.

✪ It can make him want to be unseen, unnoticed, disappear from view, sink into the ground.

✪ It can make him think poorly, and physical co-ordination can go too. So the child becomes clumsy.

✪ It can make him not hesitate to move into telling lies to avoid another shaming attack.

✪ Shame stops play, joy, humour, the wish to explore, the wish to learn. These are all expansive things.

✪ Shame freezes everything: love, joy, all wanting to reach out to others. It freezes expansiveness. It freezes spontaneity and precipitates moving into a tight, self-protective position. 'He starts to feel that it will be safer not to do the things he wants to do: "Stay in the corner, be modest, and most of all, do not be conspicuous…"' (Horney, 1977, p 213)

✫ Shame is a lethal discourager.

✫ Shame is not a mild emotion. It is feeling acutely painful, ill-at-ease with oneself.

✫ Shame denotes a state of self-damnation… 'To be ashamed is to feel devoid of goodness, full of sin, and utterly reprehensible' (Berke, 1987, p320).

✫ Being shamed is a shock to body as well as mind. If you focus on it, you can feel very vividly the awful rush of stress chemicals in your body and brain. In fact Sartre described shame as 'an immediate shudder which runs through me from head to foot without any discursive preparation' – a disruption so powerful that it felt to him like an internal haemorrhage (Sartre, 1956, p222).

✫ There is often a devastating aloneness in the moment of shame. As Nathanson says, 'In the moment of shame we feel shorn not just from the other but from all possible others' (1987, p9).

✫ Children who have felt deeply shamed can become depressed. Research shows that common childhood origins of depression often include early shaming. It is now accepted that the primitive, biologically based emotion of shame is a central component of severe depressive pathologies in both children (Izard & Schwartz, 1986) and adults (Gilbert, 1992; Lewis, 1987).

Simon, aged twelve

Twelve-year-old Simon had been brought up by a very disciplinarian father who shamed Simon into a fearful compliance. Simon never put a foot wrong, and he would never speak out in the classroom, or put himself forward in any way. Simon told his counsellor that he hoped he would get to the end of this life by hiding in the undergrowth (metaphorically speaking), with the fewer people noticing him the better. This is a natural response to repeated shaming – why risk further shaming through exposure, when you can hide and remain unscathed by another's reprisals?

Without counselling, the life of the shamed child can remain paralysed right into adulthood; the child never becoming what he could so easily have become with more encouragement and less discouragement. Without help, all too often these shamed children tragically settle for very little, because it does not risk the shaming eye.

Shaming a child through cold looks and stony silences

The young child has neither the cognitive nor the emotional resources to defend against contemptuous shaming looks of their parent or other significant adult. Basically, these inputs are just too strong. The right brain is genetically programmed to pick up emotional atmospheres in 30 milliseconds. Where an adult may have build up years of left-brain defences against this, young children do not have this luxury. They are still too wide open and so very vulnerable. Children pick up all too easily on the intensity of the unspoken hate or rage seen in the look of an adult, or felt in their cold silences. Shaming silences can be even more lethal than shaming words. They linger in the air far longer, polluting all in their wake.

John, aged eight

John, a boy of eight, could not look people in the eye. He was very withdrawn at school, and a loner in the playgroup. He often sat and just stared out of the window. Someone said it was as if he had all the life drained out of him. John also suffered from nightmares. His only interest seemed to be horror movies.

John's mother had fallen into a bitter anger after her husband ran off with another woman. She had never grieved his going. She told John that he reminded her of his father. The mornings were the worst. John would get up and his mother would be angrily cleaning the house (although it was already clean). She would not say anything or indeed look at John. When John went into play therapy, he made up a story called 'The killing of the vacuum cleaner'. He suddenly came to life when he acted out his story on paper, smashing up the vacuum cleaner. (There is always rage under shame.) He said he loathed vacuum cleaners, their terrible noise, against the background of his mother's silences. In a moment of insight he said, 'I think my mother does her screaming through the hoover.'

Shaming a child's body and its natural result of body-hate

Many stages of growing up involve mess and accidents around natural bodily functions. If these are met with criticism, the child quickly learns to feel that he or she is fundamentally wrong in some way, often without understanding why. If a baby or child is given the message that s/he is dirty, smelly, or disgusting, then these opinions are all too easily internalised, and form a view of the self. Similarly, if the infant's body products are greeted with disgust, or if toilet-training mistakes are used against the infant as shaming weapons, then the child can grow up with a legacy of bodily shame and hate. He may develop a tortured relationship with his body as described in Chapter 1.

Some children are often closely observed while sitting on the potty. When the mother looks at a child in this situation with love in her eyes, welcoming his products – which the child often shows his mother with pride – the child can develop an early confidence in his capacity to do and to make. However, a mother may look at the child on the potty with frustration, disgust, or impatience, with a sense of 'Hurry up, don't waste my time.', or criticism for not 'performing'. If a negative atmosphere is created, the child may develop a deep sense of ashamed body-consciousness. When children sense that they provoke disgust in the other, they often learn to see themselves as disgusting.

Similar psychological damage can be done by critical remarks when a child first plays with his genitals, has his first sexual encounter, or starts to develop in puberty, etc. Michael Jackson talks most poignantly about his trauma of appearing in front of thousands of people when he was an adolescent. He was sure they would be focusing on his spotty face, and find his spots disgusting, because his father had so dreadfully shamed him about them. This example serves to show just how lethal shame can be for self-esteem and body image.

> *Sally:* 'I just remember things like blood and how I used to hide my… I couldn't cope with menstrual blood when I was a child, and how I used to hide these sanitary towels in the wardrobe, and… how my mother found them one day and just called me a filthy slut… and knickers, you know, that you had to wash the blood out of. She just found them one day and called me a filthy slut. Oh I don't want everybody to know this, because it's bad enough knowing that you've done all these things, without other people knowing about it.'

> *MJ:* 'Know, and make you feel that they think you're filthy.'
>
> *Sally:* 'Yes, I do think they'll think I'm filthy.'
> (Jackson & Williams, 1994, pp32–3)

As a result of being shamed, the child may develop all manner of tormented interactions with his own body – cutting, eating disorders, and social phobias – for example, not wanting to be seen eating in public, or sunbathing, or going to a public toilet. For some, such torment can extend to their sexuality: sex is only fully enjoyed if it is based on phantasies of submission, dominance and body humiliation (eroticising shame is a classic defence and way of coping with childhood experiences of shame).

A child is all the more susceptible to the legacy of a deeply troubled body-self if his family culture was devoid of natural, loving physical contact – spontaneous hugs and cuddles. These give the child a very different message about the value and loveliness of his body.

From certain forms of discipline to low self-esteem

> Punishing causes organisms to close themselves in, freezing and withdrawing from their surroundings. Reward causes organisms to open themselves up and out toward their environment, approaching it, searching it… This fundamental duality is apparent in a creature as simple as a sea anemone… The circumstances surrounding the sea anemone determine what its entire organism does: open up to the world like a blossoming flower – at which point water and nutrients enter its body and supply it with energy – or close itself in a contracted flat pack, small, withdrawn, and nearly imperceptible to others. (Damasio, 1996, pp78–9)

Some children suffer from low self-worth because of the frequency of critical statements in the family home in contrast to the infrequency of loving, appreciative statements. While the criticism is always spoken, the praise is too often withheld. Heavy criticism is the expected parent–child interaction – a way of life – the children 'under attack' for much of the time. Because of a family atmosphere of blame and fault-finding, some children grow up to believe that frequent and damning criticism between people is the norm.

Some children are criticised unfairly for not managing something they cannot yet do developmentally. For example, Stevie, aged one, was told off very severely for crying for his Mummy in St Paul's Cathedral during the carol service. His father said, 'Stevie, you are spoiling it for everyone.' Similarly, children may be criticised for being selfish long before they are actually developmentally able to show concern and awareness for the needs of others. (In terms of neurobiology, their pre-frontal cortex is not yet developed enough for this capacity.) Piaget talks of the human developmental stage when the child's thought is primarily egocentric: the young child is not able to take into account another person's point of view. Indeed, socialised thought often does not develop until the age of seven or eight.

Why so many children who have been shamed and scared into good behaviour will never retaliate

This passage is a very astute and beautifully expressed picture of why many children who have been shamed and scared into good behaviour never retaliate:

> It is quite a different thing to be the recipient of a shaming attack from his mother than to be a deliverer of one. Although [he] may be mortified, that is, shamed near death, it would be another matter indeed to deliver back to mother such a blow... To say something to mother of equal violence invites two opposite sorts of disaster. If the shaming blow is of mortal intensity, and delivered to the vital spot, mother may die, leaving [him] bereft and just as abandoned, as [he] felt when [he was] attacked. On the other hand, if the blow is not mortal, mother may get very angry, and loose even more punishment on [his] head. In most families a child learns to suffer humiliation in silence. It is even possible that this early experience of repressing [anger from shame] acts as a training ground for the later development of depression.
> (Nathanson, 1987, p254)

As the quotation suggests, disciplining a child through shame is often far too effective in breaking a child's will. He learns how lethal shaming is because he feels the agony of it at the hands of his parent or teacher. He fears it may be damaging to his mother (of whom he may be very frightened, yet whom he desperately needs), so he cannot use the weapon of shame. Also, he is terrified that if he uses this all-too-powerful weapon of shame, it will be like dropping bombs: there may be some terrible retaliation which could frighten and shame him all over again.

Stella, aged seven

Stella's mother used shaming to discipline her daughter. Stella was referred to therapy because she was so quiet and withdrawn, with a very poor opinion of herself and, as the teachers said, she was 'worryingly good'. Stella said to the therapist, 'I don't understand why I can never say anything against my mother. I can't even say, "I don't like your skirt."' For the first time, Stella was becoming aware that she was never able to criticise in the face of being criticised, or to fight back in any way.

If a child is not helped in childhood, this total paralysis of freewill, protest and reciprocal dialogue can be difficult to overcome in adult life, as the next poem explores.

Nearest and Dearest

You burst with shout, I swallow hard
No drain to flush away your hate
It's hanging in the air like a forgotten scarf
That no one quite dared throw away.
You shriek, and throw your rant
Against my silent backdrop,
It highlighted you well.
Your face full-fixed with soured time,
The slit of mouth, too long unkissed
Shrinking still, a single line of tight
From all the bitter years.

I, a faceless blank,
Held in unbreathing self,
Needed then, but now
Like a trained rat who knows no other way,
It's hard to do anything else.

Margot Sunderland

How a child's self-critic is born

> Why did you call him Tortoise, if he wasn't one?' Alice asked. 'We called him Tortoise because he taught us', said the Mock Turtle angrily: 'Really you are very dull! You ought to be ashamed of yourself for asking such a simple question,' added the Gryphon; and then they both sat silent and looked at poor Alice, who felt ready to sink into the earth. (Carroll, 1970, p102)

Children easily take in critical messages. These are often passively accepted as being 'the truth', rather than simply someone's opinion.

✫ 'You're stupid.'

✫ 'You're no good.'

✫ 'You're so clumsy.'

Such statements may have been expressed to the child verbally or non-verbally. The child then replays these messages to himself in his head as if they were the truth, therefore giving them great power. So the shaming or critical adult can all too quickly become a self-critic in the child's head. This means that the child who has been shamed continues to shame himself. 'Shame can be activated by an actual person or an internal figure. The latter are probably the most devastating' (Berke, 1987, p329).

In other words, this self-critic can be even more ruthless than the original shaming critical adult. When the child's inner critic is speaking, he says things in his head like, 'That was stupid.'; 'Oh no, don't do that – it will only go wrong.'; 'What a silly idea.'; 'You don't know anything.' 'You always mess it up anyway.'; 'You're rubbish at drawing/reading/writing.' etc. Hearing this voice of discouragement in his head is enough to severely interrupt the child from being spontaneously expressive and creative in his life.

Children who meet too much discouragement in their life do not have an equally strong self-comforter or self-advocate in their self-talk through which to speak back to the self-critic. Unlike real courts, the courtroom in their head has no fair, impartial judge and jury, or compassionate, supportive friend, only the condemner.

One view is that some things said to children under the age of five are as powerful as if they were under hypnosis. This is because the child has no long-standing knowledge of himself, others or the world to clearly and securely pronounce them wrong. (This can be reinforced by being told that adults, particularly parents, are always right.)

> Only the crap… you know, it sticks,
> The crap you have to fight.
> You're sometimes nothing but a walking shithouse.
> (Pinter, from *Message*, 1991, p43)

Without essential self-awareness gained in child counselling or therapy, children do not usually hear their critical self-talk. They do not move from the self-criticism of 'You are really bad and selfish.' to thinking, 'Ah yes, I'm replaying the voice of my father who said this to me when I was three.' If a child had an awareness of what he was doing to himself, he would have far more choice about stopping this awful reindoctrination. Sadly, what usually happens instead is that the child hears the critical inner voices as if they were the truth, having entirely forgotten who said them in the first place.

A further problem is that these internal critical messages often get embellished over time, becoming far more harsh and critical than the original messages. For example, 16-year-old Laurie's early message from his father of 'I don't think you are really cut out to be clever like your brother.' changed over time into the lethal self-talk of 'You're so thick and brain-dead! You stupid thickie! See, you've blown it again!' It was causing him severe learning difficulties. He would feel paralysed at school, particularly in mathematics.

The following extract from *Great Expectations* describes young Pip's humiliation by Estella, and serves to show just how quickly a child learns to put himself down in the face of the criticism of others:

'He calls the Knaves Jacks, this boy!' said Estella with disdain, before our first game was out. 'And what coarse hands he has! And what thick boots!' I had never thought of being ashamed of my hands before; but I began to consider them a very indifferent pair. Her contempt for me was so strong, that it became infectious, and I caught it. (Dickens, 1995, p51)

Hence, being tormented by critical voices in their head all the time, it is like having their mind populated by persecutors. Life is all too easily reduced to a miserable affair.

> Blush, blush, thou lump of foul deformity...
> (Lady Anne in *Richard III*, I, 2, 57)

Abuse and self-esteem: why some children who have known abject cruelty, physical or sexual abuse, think they deserve it

> The 'dog that didn't deserve to be a child', the child who 'didn't come out of his mother's stomach', and the array of 'worthless' people who otherwise would have been loved by their 'noble' parents all attempted to explain and justify their perception of their parents' hostile and aggressive feelings by blaming themselves. (Bloch, 1978, p 229)

Where a parent is repeatedly cruel, many children conclude that they deserve it. So often the child thinks, 'I must be so bad to be treated like this', or 'I can't be worth much to be treated like this.' If they were to let themselves know that Mummy or Daddy, whom they need so much, was cruel to them, how would they live with this fact? For so many children in this situation, it is unthinkable to acknowledge that their parent – the person who is supposed to be keeping you safe in the world, is actually very dangerous. The thinking often goes something like this:

> If you are bad, I would reject you, but I can't because I need you. If I am good, how can you be bad to me if you are good? The reason you are bad to me is because I must be bad.' (Armstrong-Perlman, 1995, p94)

If the child sees himself as bad, it leaves him free to see his father or mother who is cruel to him as good. Once the 'cruelty' of his parent is split off like this the child has found a way of controlling the awful situation, but at a very high price. Now he is a despicable child, worthy of these 'punishments' from his parent. Fairbairn (psychoanalyst) expresses this well, in terms of it being intolerable for the child to contemplate that he lives in a bad-parent-world:

It is better to be a sinner in a world ruled by God than to live in a world ruled by the Devil. A sinner in a world ruled by God may be bad; but there is always a certain sense of security to be derived from the fact that the world around is good – 'God's in His heaven – All's right with the world!' and in any case there is always a hope of redemption. In a world ruled by the Devil the individual may escape the badness of being a sinner; but he is bad because the world around him is bad. Further, he can have no sense of security and no hope of redemption. The only prospect is one of death and destruction. (Fairbairn, 1952a, p67)

Figure 5 The effect of abuse or cruelty on self-esteem

'If you are bad, I would reject you but I can't because I need you. If I am good, how can you be bad to me if you are good? The reaon you are bad to me is because I must be bad' (Armstrong-Perlman, 1995, p94)

And similarly, Rowe: 'They were wicked gods. Then suddenly we were afraid. They were the only gods we had. If we destroyed them we would be alone. So we buried our rage and said instead, "My gods are good. I have perfect parents"' (Rowe, 1988 p45).

The problem is that the cruelty and 'badness' doesn't go away. It's just transferred to an internal theatre, as Armstrong-Perlman (1995, p94) puts it. In the internal theatre of the child's mind, the child takes on 'the badness' and feels self-hate. This leaves him free to love his cruel parent. This 'pact with the devil' can often be seen very clearly in a child's play.

Simon, aged four
Simon, whose mother had repeatedly beaten him, said he felt he was so bad that someone should put him in prison. He fiercely protected his mother, and told his therapist repeatedly how much he loved his mother. 'But can we play the Bad Witch game again, because I had another nightmare about her last night?' The 'split-off' cruelty that floated around in his 'internal theatre' came out regularly in his play.

Figure 6 Toby seeing 'Satan's Son' in the mirror.

Toby, aged eleven
Toby was tied to a chair by his father when he was naughty. Even so, he couldn't say anything against his father. When he looked at himself in the mirror he would repeatedly say to himself, 'I am Satan's son.' He felt he was evil. Logically speaking, he did equate his parent with 'Satan'. But he totally disowned this logic when asked to look at it.

Jeffrey, aged eight
Jeffrey had been hit on his hands by his step-father when he was naughty. Sometimes they would bleed as a result. When he made a mistake at school, Jeffrey would hit his own knuckles on to his desk, so his hands bled. He never had a bad word to say about his step-father.

As we see in this last example, the kind of physical punishment a child receives from an adult can actually be replayed by the child in some form of self-inflicted abuse. The body holds its memories, and the punishment can continue in the absence of the punisher. Something so deeply entrenched as this in a child's body-mind needs counselling or therapy.

Tina, aged twelve
Some abused children feel an insistent need to be punished for their 'wickedness'. Tina had always felt guilty for 'causing' her father to sexually abuse her, until one day, out of the blue, she smashed ten windows. She cried tears of relief – 'Now at last perhaps I'll be locked up.' she said, 'It's kind of what I've been waiting for.'

Sally, aged thirteen
She had been taken into care as she was being badly beaten. Sally started stealing quite blatantly from people's handbags, and went into a secure unit. She said it was a relief to know that other people would now be safe from her, and that at last she was getting the punishment she deserved.

The following passage expresses with great clarity just how vital it is that abused children, who see themselves as bad, meet with empathy and compassion as opposed to yet more harshness or criticism:

> If a child feels he has committed some terrible crime, and meets with a parent who does not share his self-appraisal of 'wicked' but instead meets a parent who is firm yet understanding and compassionate, then the child's terrible belief of himself is lessened, as there will be a mismatch between the persecuting parent in his head and the actual parent who is far more benign in his external reality. But if he feels wicked, plagued by frightening feelings and fantasies of himself as a monster and then meets a parent who hits him or looks at him with contempt, then he feels this confirms his inner reality. His fantasies about himself as a monster remain and are often strengthened as a result of this 'crucial exchange'. (Greenberg & Mitchell, 1983, p11).

Similarly, children who have been sexually abused can feel deeply flawed as human beings. Although they have been used as objects for the abuser's pleasure, in an attempt to reason it out to themselves, they often take on the 'badness' of the abuser, and see it as their own. Thus many child incest survivors think the whole situation is their fault, and that they were in some way responsible for the abuse happening in the first place. As Blume says:

> The child victim of incest feels soiled and spoiled. She feels contaminated by the dirty act of incest that she 'permitted' or even asked for. Feeling dirty becomes a part of her character. (Blume, 1990, p113)

This is particularly the case when the abuser is a parent, where it can be intolerable to believe that this person, who is so needed and loved, has sexually abused you.

Gemma, aged thirteen

Gemma had been sexually abused by an uncle for many years. She had recently begun cutting her arms and legs with a bread knife. She felt she deserved to suffer the pain. She wrote the following story:

'Once upon a time there was a very beautiful tree, but it was chopped down one day and made into pulp, and then it became paper and then it was used as toilet paper.' This is a vivid image of how worthless she felt, a total destruction of any goodness (the beautiful tree) she once had, now reduced to a terrible state of degradation.

The power of negative touch on a child's self-esteem

And when you get a slap – well then you're simply weighed down by the awareness of the filth you are being rubbed in. (Dostoevsky, 1991, p12)

When a child is hit or beaten, he can all too easily develop a sense of self based upon toughness and roughness. He will be far more likely to experience himself as brutal or 'hard', hating or disrespecting his body. He can carry on a very troubled and tormented relationship with his body – such as cutting, smoking, unsafe sex or substance abuse. Being beaten or hit gives a child the message that 'My body is not worthy of respect. It is to be abused, violated, and hit, and that's OK.' If a child is hit or physically abused in some other way, such as being thrown down the stairs, he may feel like a 'thing' rather than a human being worthy of respect. Extreme cases of being treated as a 'thing' instead of a person can lead to psychopathic tendencies later in life. Other people are then seen as objects too, rather than people worthy of the utmost care and concern. 'It's OK to hurt objects.' goes their reasoning, just as they themselves have been hurt.

Tragically, too many children who are persistently hurt or hit have nothing with which to contrast this harshness: no experience of tender or gentle touch, no calm holding, which could make them see that harsh treatment of their body is *not* OK and so move into justified protest.

'Now, I give you fair warning,' shouted the Queen, stamping on the ground as she spoke; 'either you or your head must be off, and that in about half no time! Take your choice!' (Carroll, 1970, p 98)

Children with low self-worth who are 'criminals in fantasy'

It is all too easy for children to take the blame for something that is actually beyond their control. For example, if parents separate or divorce, a child may fantasise that it was his fault. Many children also have a tendency to feel responsibility for things going wrong, or painful events, from an occurrence as trivial as breaking a vase (which may in fact have been done by the cat), to the illness of a sibling. This is because young children are not yet fully grounded in reality, and their imagination is extremely vivid and open.

Children can easily have omnipotent fantasies and make illogical connections. 'Because I did X, then Y happened, therefore I am responsible.' Imagining doing something, or wanting to do something, such as killing or hurting someone, can sometimes feel *as though they have actually done it*. This is called magical thinking. When their imaginings coincide with something awful happening in real life, they mistakenly connect the one with the other – such as the boy whose father had a car accident the day he wished his father dead because he had shouted at him for his messy bedroom. The thought process goes something like this: 'If I wanted him dead and then he died, I must have killed him.'

In fact, some adults lead a guilt-ridden life and then later (often with the help of therapy or counselling) realise that they have been doing this to punish themselves, due to an irrational belief dating back to early childhood. One woman, for example, believed that at 10 she was responsible for not keeping her father alive. Ever since, she had made sure that everything good that happened in her life she sabotaged as self-inflicted punishment. She felt she was a very bad person indeed.

This terrible burden of guilt and shame is particularly common in families where there is a belief in fundamental evil, and where there are strict punishments and a great deal of disapproval. As the writer Margaret Drabble states:

I recall that I had convinced myself that I had committed what I called 'the sin against the Holy Ghost'. I didn't know what this was, but I had heard or read somewhere that it was unpardonable and therefore I was convinced that I had committed it. Whatever the cause, the effect was real. I moped, I wept, lumps of my hair dropped out. (Drabble, 1996, p91)

Gillian, aged six
Gillian was playing her new plastic trumpet in the garden. While she was playing, the man next door had a heart attack in his garden. She saw him fall to the ground. She thought she was responsible because she was being too noisy at the time.

Julian, aged six
Julian thumped his sister, and next day she got chickenpox. He was too young to understand what this meant, but saw her ill in bed, thought she was going to die, and felt he was responsible for her condition.

Now hopefully a child 'criminal in fantasy' meets with a reassuring adult. But if he doesn't, there can be untold psychological damage. Children need to know that thoughts and imaginings like wanting someone dead, or wanting someone to suffer, are not against the law, and that if you went to a police station and 'owned up' to having a hateful, revengeful thought about your little brother, you would be told politely to leave the police station.

Children who have been told they are 'bad blood'

> ...I shut my doors on that dark guilt,
> I bolt the door, each door I bolt.
> Blood quickens, gonging in my ears:
> The panther's tread is on the stairs,
> Coming up and up the stairs.'
> (Plath, from *Pursuit*, 1981, p23)

Obviously, if children are told they are of bad blood, it can do untold damage to their self-esteem. Some parents can be heard to say publicly, 'I gave birth to a monster.' Some adults, even in the twenty-first century, still believe that some children are indeed born bad, despite all the neurobiological evidence in the last decade that proves beyond doubt that it is parent–child interactions that are so deeply influential in terms of whether a child moves into anti-social behaviour or not. After tragic events, such as the James Bulger case, people are quick to call some children evil, as they were with witch hunts in the Middle Ages. Despite one hundred years of psychotherapy, there is still often a reluctance to look at the parent–child interactions that these deeply troubled children have suffered, and which brought them to this horrific breaking point.

Children who suffer low self-worth because of a very strict religious upbringing

> Thou shall beat him [the child] with the rod, and shalt deliver his soul from hell. (*Proverbs* 23: 14)

Some children with a strict religious upbringing suffer from low self-worth, especially where God is made out to be a very fierce judge. Where children grow up with an (Old Testament) concept of the wrath of God (who punishes with very violent means), and when they are all too familiar with images of Hell and Damnation, they may live with a feeling of the sword of Damocles hanging perpetually over their head. This can be made worse by having a very strict or authoritarian parent, 'Not only Daddy thinks I'm bad for taking the last sweetie without asking, but God does as well.'

Some children react to the concept of 'original sin' by thinking that they are born bad and therefore must atone in penance; that they must constantly struggle to be seen as good in the eyes of what they see as a harsh, authoritarian god; that they must ask for his mercy and forgiveness. Children are often deeply affected by tales of plagues, fire and brimstone for sinners, the shameful fall from grace, and human wickedness. For some children, these stories are too alive in their imagination. They are all too open to seeing themselves as miserable sinners.

Some children carry an image in their heads of an 'all-seeing' god who lives in the sky, who looks down and sees everything they do wrong, and is ready to punish their wrongdoings with awful events. Some children, with such a religious background, still cower before an avenging godhead (all too vivid in their imagination) right into adulthood. They can be left with a legacy of shame that blights their life and self-worth.

When feelings of worthlessness come from being the family scapegoat

The child can be the 'carrier' of all manner of family problems, relationship difficulties, feelings of hate, resentment, frustration, etc. He is then labelled 'the problem in the family'. A child may be scapegoated in the sense that he is seen to represent all the things the parents dislike in themselves or in each other – such as greed, laziness, or a quick temper. Children are such easy targets for displacement and projection. A child may be labelled 'the aggressive one', or 'the one who's always so greedy and selfish', and so become a convenient carrier for all the disowned or denied aspects of other family members.

The effect of bullying on a child's self-esteem

> His laugh thumped my body
> (Hughes, from *Sacrifice*, 1994, p125)

Bullying is particularly psychologically scarring for a child who harboured feelings of worthlessness prior to being bullied. Being cast out in the playground – 'We don't want to play with you, you smell, you're dirty and horrible, you're a fatty, your mother's a prostitute; go away…' – can be devastating to the child whose self-worth is already shaky. If, however, a child has laid down strong foundations of self-worth, as described previously, bullying is likely to make him feel angry, or fearful, but not worthless. He is also more likely to seek help, for he knows he is worth far better treatment and respect than this. Children who have learnt to associate grown-ups with comfort and understanding will also go and seek help to stop the abuse, before it has had any long-term damaging effects on their self-esteem.

> Do not call the tortoise unworthy because she is not something else. (Whitman, 1995, p16)

WHAT TO SAY AND HOW TO BE WITH CHILDREN WHO THINK THEY ARE WORTHLESS

Important psychological messages for children who think they are worthless

Find age-appropriate language for the statements below. For some children it will help if you draw a picture to convey the messages:

✵ All people are prone to feel that they are bad rather than good.

✵ 'You can't blame anyone for walking all over you – you can only know that you are not getting out of the way.' (Jeffers, 1995, p72)

✵ 'If you stop people oppressing, hurting or torturing you, you are doing them a favour.' (Clarkson, 1988, p85)

✵ People will treat you the way you allow them to treat you.

✵ 'We may choose to grow, to stagnate, or to decline, and in a world where there is little encouragement to grow, most of us may not do it very much or at all.' (Rowan, 1986, p13)

✵ 'An altruistic act is to prevent others from hurting you. The masochist helps the persecutor on the road to damnation. Cruelty is demeaning to both parties.' (Clarkson, 1988, p93)

✵ Some children think feeling good about themselves is about having the latest trainers or the latest video game. But this feeling good only lasts for a very short time. You can only feel really good about yourself for a long, long time, if you know someone really, really likes you.

The deadly sins, or rather common human traits: what to say to a child to move him on from shame to self-compassion

Throughout history, people have tried to make grown-ups and children feel bad and guilty for having certain feelings. These feelings are not bad. Rather, people usually have these feelings because they are hurting in some way.

Tick if you ever feel any of these feelings.

Greed ☐

'I'm so greedy, I just stuff my mouth all the time.' (Paul, aged nine)

Figure 7a Greed

What to say to the child:
Did you know that people often eat too much because they want to change the feelings they are feeling. They use food for comfort, like you get from lovely cuddles. Some children eat too much because they are unhappy and some food can make you feel better for a while. Some children use food and sweeties because they are not getting enough cuddles and comfort from kind grown-ups.

Sloth ☐

'I am just a lazy slob. Mummy tells me I am.' (Sarah, aged thirteen)

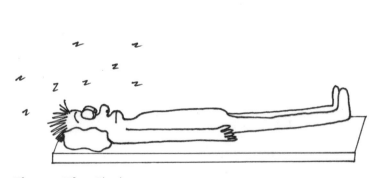

Figure 7b Sloth

What to say to the child:
Did you know that people are often 'lazy' because they are very sad or fed up? When you are very, very sad or fed up, you often don't have enough energy in your brain or your body to get up and think what you might want to do. Sometimes people are 'lazy' because they feel they are rubbish, so anything they do would be rubbish too. Because of this, they don't want to do anything, and so watching TV or staying in bed feels like the safest thing to do.

Envy ☐
'I am such a horrible person, whenever one of my friends gets something good in her life, I hope it goes wrong for her.' (Rufus, aged ten)

What to say to the child:
Did you know that lots of people feel this at some times in their lives? It's because it can hurt real bad to feel the unfairness of 'Why didn't this happen to me?' Life isn't fair like that, and so it can hurt you if you feel good things always happen to other people, and not to you. If you are feeling this a lot about your life, and about the nice things that happen to other people, it's good to tell a kind adult who has the time to listen, because telling about hurting like this can really help to make you feel better.

Figure 7c Envy

Pride ☐
'I can never say sorry. It would make me feel like a right goon.' (Paul aged twelve)

What to say to the child:
Did you know that people can become proud like this because at some time, someone made them feel small and rubbish? So if they say sorry, it feels like someone will rub their nose in what they did.

Figure 7d Pride

Anger ☐

'I'm an angry person. Other people can do kind things. I can't, I just feel so cross all the time.' (Sophie, aged nine)

Figure 7e Anger

What to say to the child:
Did you know that lots of people get angry because when they were little, no-one helped them to feel calm – so now when they get angry, they just don't know how to calm down? Their brain doesn't know and their body doesn't know either. But people called therapists and counsellors can help you feel calm. And sometimes people feel angry because it's far easier than letting themselves know that they are actually feeling hurt, or very sad. Are you really hurt or sad about something that happened or is happening to you in your life. Do you think you are using anger to cover up your hurt?

Covetousness ☐

'I always want what he has. I am never happy with what I have.' (Simon, age ten, about his brother)
'I can never seem to be happy that he has got something nice for him, like new trainers, without wanting it for me. I am just so horrible.' (Philip, age fourteen, about his best friend)

Figure 7f Covetousness

What to say to the child:
Did you know that when children feel like this about objects and things, it's often because they are hurting inside about something entirely different. Fights with brothers and sisters for example, over something they've got that you want, are often actually a cover up for feelings about people. They are often about very painful feelings that this brother or sister of yours is getting more attention and love from Mummy or Daddy than you are. These painful feelings about the people in your life, just get put on feelings about things in your life. In fact all the chocolates, trainers, books, game boys, videos, cars, clothes, pocket money etc. in the world wouldn't make you feel full up of good things, if you feel that someone else is getting more love and attention than you, from the people you really need to love and want you.

It is crazy saying to a child with low self-worth, 'You've just got to learn to love yourself more.'

A child with low self-worth cannot just learn to love himself more. Self-esteem isn't something you can get from yourself. Self-esteem comes from interactions with other people. Some books advocate thinking positively – but self-esteem is far more than thinking differently. It is about *feeling differently*, literally a different biochemical balance in your brain. It is about belief, and feeling deep down that you are really OK as a person, because you have felt yourself to be profoundly OK with an important person in your life, and seen your loveliness reflected back to you in their eyes. Thinking new things may help, but it is icing on the cake for a child who has never felt he can engender love in the people who really matter to him.

The vital role of praise and encouragement in interrupting the process of the child establishing a resident self-critic in their mind

Unlike an adult, a young child is still forming a sense of self and self-worth. Criticisms and put-downs, although very painful, may not yet have formed themselves into an immovable resident self-critic in the child's mind. Take the following as an example:

Toby, aged six
Therapist: 'Wow, that's a really clever thought!'
Toby: 'No, I'm thick. My Mummy thinks I'm thick. Am I thick?'

Toby is still able to question whether his internalising of his mother's criticism is correct or not. His question about his own stupidity shows he is still open to it not being true. In fact, by the end of the therapy, Toby said, 'I have drawn a beautiful butterfly. It is a bit like me actually.'

The following quotation shows how therapy (and/or other significant adult intervention) can feel enabling in this way:

> If my therapist really gets what it is like inside me and helps me see that I am like this, not because of some inherent badness, but because of the inevitable laws of cause and effect, a different attitude towards myself becomes possible and with it comes the possibility of change. (Kahn, 1991)

In fact warm encouraging adults can enable a child to replace the critical inner voice with a compassionate one.

Situation – child getting his homework wrong:
'What a shame you didn't get that bit right, because I know you really wanted to. Never mind. Hey, you're probably not working at your best right now. How about going for a walk and coming back later?'

As opposed to, 'You stupid fool. Wrong again! You're pathetic.'

Positive self-esteem doesn't mean you feel great about yourself all the time. It means that when you do feel ashamed, incompetent or inadequate you can manage these feelings well and be nice to yourself about it, not critical.

Children need six 'positives' for every 'negative', to maintain healthy self-esteem

> So farewell – to the little good you bear me.
> Farewell, a long farewell…
> (Cardinal Wolsey in *Henry VIII* 3 (2), pp351–2)

In order for a child to develop self-worth, for every one criticism there need to be at least six statements of praise. Many families fall well below this. Sue Jenner, author of *The Parent–Child Game* (1999), has clearly stated that a parent or teacher is setting up a child for psychological damage if they give a child anything less that six praises for any one criticism.

How to discipline a child in a way that leaves their self-worth intact

> How good it felt to have someone care enough about me to tell me in a nice way, I was doing something wrong. (Schneider, 1987, p204)

Socialising a child is something every parent has to do. There is no avoiding it. Children are not born socially adapted. And yet it is an art to socialise a child in ways that will not damage his self-esteem. In his excellent book, *Building The Bonds of Attachment* (1988), Dan Hughes has written extensively about how to confront a child without damaging his feelings of self-worth in any way. In fact his disciplining techniques also enable a child to think more about his actions, rather than just acting impulsively. Hughes uses the concepts of empathy, 'choices' and 'consequences'. Here are some examples:

Philip, aged four, hits Carl, aged three

'Hey, Philip, that was a bad choice you just made hitting Carl. Let's look at other choices now, so that when you get cross, you can do something about it that doesn't get you into trouble and stops hurting other people's bodies, which is never OK.'

This is so different from the destructive criticism such as *'That's it, Philip.'* (smack) *'See what it feels like. You lousy good-for-nothing. And go and say sorry to Carl too – you loathsome toad.'*

In the face of defiance – choices, not commands

Parent: 'We have to clear your toys up now.'

Child: 'Shan't.'

Parent: 'I know you sometimes really really hate having to do what I say, particularly when you are busy playing, but we do have to clear your toys up now.'

Child: 'Shan't. I'm off to ride my bike.'

Parent: 'Shame that you are making that choice, because the consequences of that are that we will have to stay in this room now until you have cleared up your toys, instead of going out to ride your bike in the park. But if that is the choice you are making, I will stay in this room with you until the toys are cleared. Let me know when you are ready to do that. I will be just sitting here reading the newspaper until you are ready.'

In the toy shop: empathy and giving the child his wishes in fantasy

Child: 'I want that Pokemon. Get it for me NOW.'

Parent: 'No, you can't take it.'

Child: 'I'm going to take the Pokemon out of the toy shop and you can't stop me.'

Parent: 'I wish that you could go. I can really see how much you want to have it. But the reality is that you have had your pocket money for this week. I wish I could wave a magic wand and say "Give George a mountain of Pokemons!" It would have been fun, if I could. It's a real shame that you decided to spend your pocket money on something else. It can feel horrible to want something so badly and not be able to have it now and have to wait until next week's pocket money.'

If the toddler persists, gently pick him up, separating him from the toy and remove him from the toy shop.

Toby, age five

Mother: 'Toby, I need to put some suntan lotion on you before you go to the beach.'

Toby: 'No way.'

Mother: 'Well, you can choose not to wear your suntan lotion but regrettably the consequences of that would be not being able to go to the beach. But I have to respect your choice that you would rather not put on the suntan lotion than go to the beach.'

Toby: (See Toby's higher brain whirring!) 'OK – the suntan lotion.'

If a child is socialised with choices and empathy, not commands, there is no likelihood of damaging his self-worth and moving him into shame. And if a child is not going to be shamed, tone is everything. Furthermore, disciplining that comes from a position of 'I'm OK. You're OK.' can help a child to develop emotionally, and to gain perspective. This sort of disciplining also ensures against a parent off-loading their own shaming childhood experiences on to their children.

How to help children express the pain of feeling worthless, through art or play

To feel worthless is to be in great pain. Part of this includes having to feel that pain all by yourself. Children who feel worthless need help from someone who will really listen to what it feels like to be them, and to heighten their self-awareness about how they came to feel like this, and how their critical self-talk is perpetuating their bad feelings. While children often find it hard to express themselves verbally, they may find it easier to do so through play. In the next chapter there are many exercises to enable a child to express and work through negative feelings about himself.

The power of positive touch on promoting a child's self-esteem

Montagu's superb book, *Touching* (1971), details a great deal of research into the effects of touch on psychological health and emotional well-being. The way a child is touched when young can be a major factor in forming feelings about himself and his body in later life. So, if a child is touched tenderly, expansively and with genuine warmth, he is far more likely to like his body-self and to feel valued. If the child knows loving, safe touch on a regular basis, he can experience himself as a tender, loving person.

PRACTICAL WAYS OF ENABLING CHILDREN TO SPEAK ABOUT AND WORK THROUGH FEELINGS OF LOW SELF-WORTH

Exercises and tasks for children who think they are worthless

This section is designed to provide a whole host of ideas to enable children to speak about their feelings of low self-worth in unthreatening, child-friendly ways. Children need help with a language for this, as do many adults! So these exercises are designed to enable children to speak about what they are feeling about themselves in creative and useful ways that lead to real insight and resolution, rather than just saying that they don't like themselves. In fact, the tasks and exercises are specifically designed to help a child to think about, and work through, his feelings in a way that can set him firmly on the path towards self-esteem.

Children often cannot speak clearly and fully in everyday language about what they are feeling, but they can show or enact, draw or play out their feelings very well indeed. However, they need to be given the right language of expression. For some this is writing; for others, drawing; for yet others it might be puppet play, or using miniature toys in a sandbox. Therefore, many of the exercises in this section offer support for creative, imaginative and playful ways of expression. There are also some tasks to ensure that you don't get into asking the child with low self-worth lots of questions, which he might find threatening. So some of the tasks just require a tick in a box, a quick colouring-in, or choosing a word or image from a selection.

Please note: The tasks and exercises are not designed to be worked through in order. Also, there are far too many to attempt them all in one go: the child could feel bombarded. So, just pick the ones you think would be right for the particular child you are working with, taking into account his age, and how defended or undefended he is about talking about his feelings of low self-worth. Instructions for the child are all shaded.

☆ When you don't like yourself

Do you feel any of these things? If you do, tick which ones:

- ◎ I feel I'm a bad person. ☐
- ◎ I don't deserve anything good in the world. ☐
- ◎ I make people unhappy, not happy. ☐
- ◎ I keep comparing myself to other children, and they are always better than me. ☐
- ◎ I feel stupid. ☐
- ◎ I'm sure people can see how horrid I am on the inside, no matter how nice I try to be on the outside. ☐
- ◎ I feel bad inside and out. ☐
- ◎ I'm rubbish, I've always known it. ☐
- ◎ Sometimes I feel like the last worm on earth. ☐
- ◎ I am nothing. ☐

Can you remember when you first thought these things about yourself? You've got it all wrong, but you probably won't think that you have. You see, children usually only feel this bad about themselves if they have not had enough appreciation and love from the people in their lives. Some grown-ups are just very bad at giving praise, others forget to. Other grown-ups are far better at telling children off than they are at giving them praise. Other grown-ups just don't like children very much. But this says a lot about the grown-up and nothing about you. These grown-ups have always had an unhappy childhood themselves.

☆ When grown-ups just make you feel worse inside

This next exercise is important in ascertaining whether a child is suffering from shame issues or not. If so, then read the last chapter in this book, called 'Considering Counselling or Therapy for children with Low Self-Worth'.

Do you ever feel any of the following things?

- ⊚ I get very worried about making mistakes. ☐
- ⊚ I often feel I can't do anything right. ☐
- ⊚ I get worried about being told off all the time ☐
- ⊚ I don't feel I have a voice. ☐
- ⊚ I feel I'm about to be found out or told off all the time, even when I haven't done anything wrong. ☐
- ⊚ I feel frightened any time a grown-up asks me to speak, in case I say something wrong. ☐
- ⊚ I often feel I've been bad in some way. ☐
- ⊚ I'm often ready to take the blame for something, because it feels like it *must* have been me, even when I know it isn't. ☐

☆ Things that make you feel awful

Which of the following is the worst for you? Tick which one or colour in the picture below. You can have more than one.

A grown-up with a very cross face telling you off.	A grown-up with a very cold and angry voice telling you off.
People laughing at you.	People ignoring you.
People calling you names.	

Figure 8

If it is none of these, but another thing, draw what it is for you in the empty box.

☆ The critical person in your head

This exercise can give both the adult and the child a sense of the people who contributed to making the child feel so awful about himself. The child then may be enabled to appreciate that he is not stupid, rubbish, etc, rather that he has swallowed whole the verbal or non-verbal messages from the grown-ups in his life. Children can realise, for example, that the cruel and harsh voices in their head saying *'How silly and selfish!'* are not in fact their own, but their father's. They can come to realise that the voices are actually simply the opinion of, say, a parent, rather than an 'absolute consensual truth' about *them*. Then they can come to let these critical opinions go, by being able to differentiate from them. *'That is what Daddy thought – I no longer share his opinion.'* Looked at another way, when the originator of an inner critic voice is identified for the first time, there is now a real and conscious choice about whether or not to play that particular 'tape' in their head any more.

- ◎ Look at the picture of the nasty critical person who lives in your head – the one who keeps telling you that you are rubbish.

- ◎ When you think of the critic who lives in your head, what are they saying? Draw or write it in the speech bubble.

- ◎ Is the person large or small, a man or a woman? Is it more than one person? You can change the drawing if you like, or draw a different drawing of your inner critic.

- ◎ What is the most horrid or frightening part of them – their mouth, their eyes, their hands, etc.?

- ◎ Are they a judge? a critic? a spoiler?

- ◎ Is there anyone in your life that your inner critic reminds you of?

- ◎ Now look at the second picture of a nice kind person in your head, one who just says kind things to you, and tells you that you are doing just fine. Write what they would be saying to you in the speech bubble, if you had a nice kind person like this in your head.

- ◎ Now draw a picture of your critic and your kind person together. Is there anything you would like the person who is kind about you to say to the person who is very critical about you?

- ◎ What would you like to do to the inner critic in your head? Draw it on the drawing.

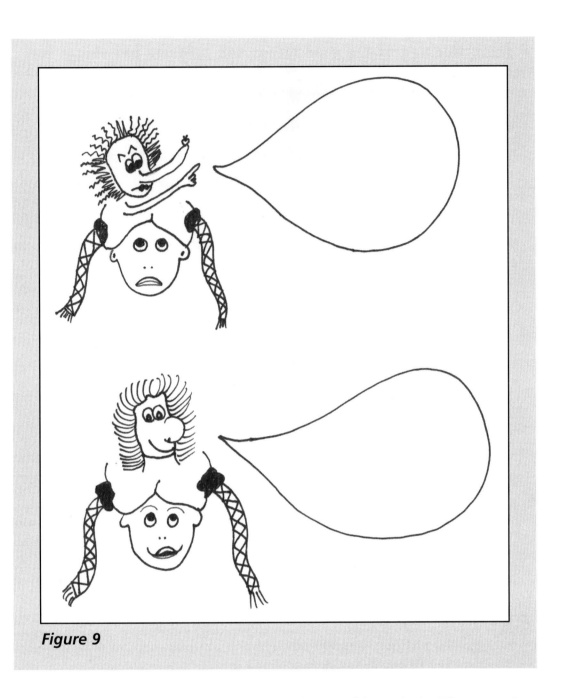

Figure 9

Children may not want to throw out their inner critic entirely. They may just want to reduce him in size, or prevent him from saying some of the things he says. Other children will wish to throw him away as he is clearly seen as 100 per cent unhelpful.

☆ When thinking of the good things can help the bad things feel smaller

- ◎ Make a list of all the things you have done that you are proud of.

- ◎ Make a list of all the things and people that make you feel good inside, rather than rubbish inside. These are people who you know really like you.

- ◎ Keep the list somewhere and look at it often. Add to it whenever anything new occurs to you. Nothing is too small to be included on your list!

☆ Warm, fuzzy people and cold, prickly ones
(taken from a story by John Steiner, 1977)

Are you getting enough good things said to you and done to you in your life? Without these it is too easy to think you are rubbish. Fill in the charts below with the good things and the bad things that happened to you in the last week:

GOOD THINGS	
IN THE LAST WEEK:	**Number of times** Do a smile for lots. Do a straight line mouth for a few. Do a sad mouth for none.
How many times has someone said they liked something about you?	
How many times has someone said they liked something you did or made?	
How many times have you been given a really nice touch – a hug, a cuddle, a nice squeeze?	
How many times have you felt really listened to?	

BAD THINGS	
IN THE LAST WEEK:	**Number of times** Do a sad mouth for lots. Do a straight line mouth for a few. Do a smile for no times.
How many times have you had bad things said about you, such as 'You are so stupid', or 'You are rubbish'?	
How many times has your body been treated roughly/badly?	
How many times have you been ignored?	
How many times have you been treated as if you didn't matter, or what you had to say didn't matter?	
How many times have you felt frightened by a grown-up?	

☆ The fairground of lovely moments when you felt special

Write or draw on the horses, some of the best times in your life, when you felt really good about yourself. (For example when you played football last week, when your Dad said he loved you, when your Mum squeezed your arm, when you won a prize.) Keep these times as treasure in your mind.

Figure 10

☆ The big wheel of bad moments

Draw or write on each of the carriages on the big wheel, the moments in your life when you felt awful, horrid or that you were rubbish. How could a kind grown-up have helped you not to feel these things. What might they have said or done.

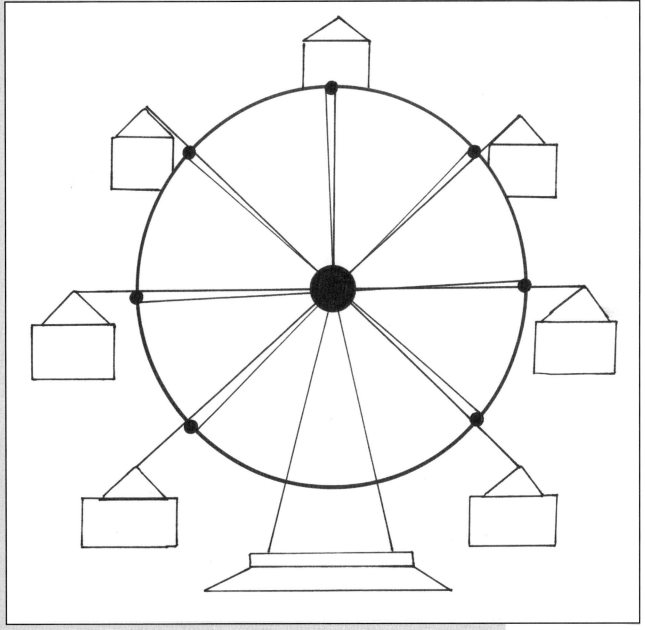

Figure 11

☆ 'If all the world's a stage, why can't I have a better part?'
(Glouberman, 1989, p239)

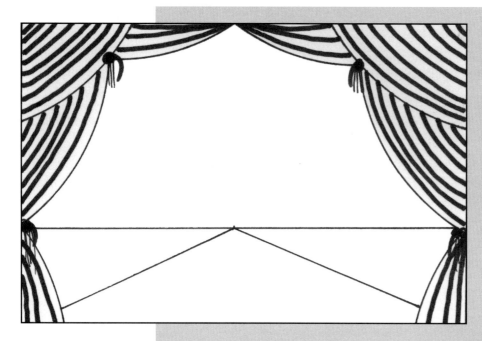

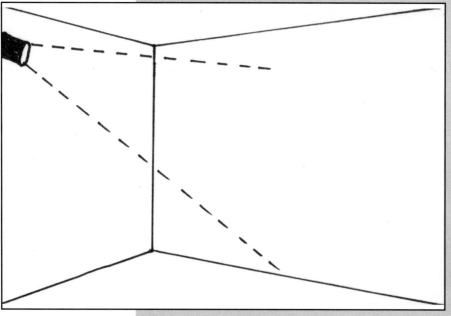

Figure 12

If you could change your life and have a better part to play: Who would you be? What would you do? Who would like you? Who would love you? Who would be your friends? What lovely things would they say about you? Draw them on the stage or film set.

What rubbishy things have people said to you, which you have believed when they were not true?

Write them in the empty box at the bottom of the page. Then write next to them what you would have liked to say back to this person, or do to this person.

✫ Flying over the Trouble Trolls

Imagine flying on a magic carpet above all your troubles. What would you be? A seagull; a golden eagle; Superman; a vulture; a pterodactyl? Draw yourself on the magic carpet in the picture. As you fly high, below you can see your Trouble Trolls. Write above each of your Trouble Trolls a worry or trouble you are carrying around in your life. (Trouble Trolls carry things like 'trouble with bullies', 'trouble with sums', 'trouble with people liking you'.) What do you feel about your worries and troubles when you are flying high above them instead of getting all muddled up in them? Colour in red, the trolls which are carrying a worry or trouble you really need some help with. This is a worry or trouble that isn't going away because it hasn't worked well trying to manage it all on your own.

Figure 13

✰ When you like yourself and when you don't

What does it feel like to be you when you like yourself?

Make a clay image of it.

Show the feeling in a movement.

Play it in music.

Draw a picture of yourself when you feel like this.

Think of someone who you like being with, someone who makes you feel good about yourself.

Use your paints to show the colours they make you feel (it might be sunny, or like a rainbow, or a clear blue sky).

What does it feel like to be you when you *don't* like yourself?

Make a clay image of it.

Show the feeling in a movement.

Play it in music.

Draw a picture of yourself when you feel like this.

☆ The rubbish things that grown-ups have said to you

Write on the pieces of rubbish, some of the hurtful things that grown-ups have called you. Example, 'You're stupid.'; 'You're not as clever as your sister.'; 'You are no good.'

See how the rubbish things they said are in the rubbish bin. They should be kept in a rubbish bin, not in your head. Are you carrying around any of these in your head?

(Did you know that often grown-ups can make you feel rubbish, because someone has made them feel rubbish?)

Figure 14

☆ The gallery of discouragers and encouragers

Some people in the world just go about making people feel bad or small or that they are rubbish. Others make people feel good about themselves.

In the gallery of encouragers, write the names of some people in your life who have made you feel good.

Figure 15a   The Gallery of Encouragers

In the gallery of discouragers write the names of some people in your life who have made you feel awful about yourself.

Figure 15b   The Gallery of Discouragers

☆ The special treasure box

Draw or write in the special box all the lovely thoughts and lovely things and lovely times, and kind things people have said, that have made you feel good about yourself, not bad. So if someone said you were good at football, you might draw a football. If someone said 'I like being your friend', draw a smile, or your friend.

Figure 16

☆ Jack-in-a-box feelings!

When someone makes you feel no good or like you are rubbish, you can feel small and tight, as if you have shrunk. Sometimes to change the horrid feelings inside you, you have got to do something big. Colour in the big thing you like best from this set of pictures, then do a movement to become it, or do a noise to be it.

◎ A whirlpool

◎ A shooting star

◎ Fireworks night

◎ Jumping in a puddle

◎ Singing in the rain

Or draw your own lovely big thing in the empty box, and then make a movement or a noise to become that.

Figure 17

☆ 'I'm not that, I'm me'

Have you ever felt horrid inside, because someone wanted you to be something or someone you are not? What did they want you to be that you weren't? Here are some things people want some children to be, when they just can't be that thing. Tick if a grown-up has ever wanted you to be one of these, or write your own example.

- ◎ A strong person who never cries. ☐
- ◎ A girl, not a boy, or a boy, not a girl. ☐
- ◎ Like an adult, when you are only a child. ☐
- ◎ Someone who is good at maths, when you hate maths. ☐
- ◎ Someone who is good at spelling, when you hate spelling. ☐
- ◎ Someone who likes a certain food, when you hate that food. ☐
- ◎ Someone who can sit very still, when you can't sit still. ☐
- ◎ Someone who has the skin colour that you don't have. ☐
- ◎ Someone who believes in something that you don't. ☐
- ◎ Someone who likes something or someone that you don't. ☐

Helping Children with Low Self-Esteem © M Sunderland & N Armstrong 2003

✩ Words that feel like a smack

Think of three things that people have said to you when they were being really angry or mean – things that were like a terrible hurt, as if you'd been smacked. Write them in the speech bubbles. Draw what it made you feel. Now draw a picture of you telling them what you think and feel about them making you feel like this.

Figure 18

CONSIDERING COUNSELLING OR THERAPY FOR CHILDREN WHO SUFFER FROM LOW SELF-ESTEEM

What's the point of counselling or therapy for a child who has to go home each night to a painful or frightening home environment?

Therapy changes the world *inside* the child's head. It is the job of the social worker to change (if necessary) the child's outer world. The world inside the child's head can be a cold, discouraging place – too bleak, too desolate, too alone. Therapy can populate the child's inner world of thoughts and feelings with images of kind people, kind thoughts, lovely memories of shared states of joy. His inner world, which is the world that colours his moment-to-moment perception, can become a far warmer world through therapy.

For children whose low self-worth has resulted from just too much shame, anger and discouragement from other people, therapy can enable them to

Figure 19 A child's inner world before therapy and after therapy

experience, on an ongoing basis, a compassionate rather than a negative response. This can have a profound effect on their self-worth and the world inside their head. So to reiterate, you may not be able to change the child's outer world – for example, make his parents less angry – but you can make his inner world a far warmer place to be. This is expressed in the beautiful lines from Neruda's poem:

> I want to do with you
> what spring does with the cherry trees.
>
> (Neruda, 1969, p43)

The therapist's response of empathy and understanding, rather than that of judgement or criticism, is for some children their first experience of real warmth and concern. Teachers have so many children that they often have no time to verbalise their compassion for a child's emotional pain, given the time that compassion often needs to be expressed well and fully.

Therapy can facilitate 'phoenix' behaviour in the child

The child who has known just too many oppressive put-downs and criticisms can start to fly when encouraged by a therapist, teacher or other very significant person. Children with low self-worth need powerful encouragement to help them to find their natural will to rise above the oppression they have known. But to unleash this, they need at least one powerful adult advocate. As Mitchell says,

> The analyst's task is to fan the embers, to re-kindle the spark. (1988, p189)

Good therapy will give a child the experience of having a voice, of being truly heard, seen and valued, which has a profound effect on self-worth

> The [therapist] pays close attention to every word I say, as if what I am saying is of the utmost importance. (Thrail, 1994, p46)

Therapy for some children with low self-worth may provide the first secure attachment relationship

As Dan Hughes says:

> [Without attachment relationships] a child cannot experience herself as being special and worthwhile. (Hughes, 1998, p82)

Therapy can enable the shamed child to build a sense of self-worth

Therapy can enable shamed children to understand what shame is and to know what is happening to them when they are feeling shamed, rather than having that awful feeling in their tummy and the terrible pain of descending into a black hole. Therapy can enable children to know when someone is trying to shame them, and what they can do about it. This can give them the resources they need to find healthy defences against shame.

If a child has been repeatedly shamed and never receives counselling or psychotherapy, or never finds a powerfully encouraging attachment figure, the scars from shame can continue for a lifetime. Such scars can deeply affect the child's feelings of potency and spontaneity, and his sense of himself as someone of value. He may shut himself off from new opportunities, not daring to go fully for something he wants in his life. Because, he reasons, it may lead to yet more shaming. Such a child can adjust his life to trying all the time to go unseen and unnoticed.

Therapy as a time to express needs and feelings that have been too dangerous and frightening to express in the past

> It's very difficult to have a feeling when Daddy is having his all the time. (Little girl whose drunk father was often in an angry state.)

In the safe environment of therapy, children often feel enough trust to dare again to express feelings and needs, which in the past have only led them to feeling unheard, rejected, frightened or criticised. Perhaps the parent has retaliated with anger or rage, or crumpled in some way. The child has then realised that the parent is too emotionally fragile or volatile for him to be able to have his feelings.

So when children from such a background know that a feeling they have experienced as too dangerous in the past, has been met with understanding, it can be an immense relief. At last their feelings have been both accepted and normalised.

Therapy can help a child who has moved into a position of submission, passivity or powerlessness to find their anger, their protest, their self-respect – their *active voice*

Access to her anger spontaneously allowed her to feel for the first time that she was living in her own life rather than adjusting to others' lives. (Orbach, 1994, p60)

Why the power of intense one-to-one attention by a therapist is such a powerful experience for children with low self-worth

Children whose parents have been unable to love them well enough, because of their own childhoods, can find it very difficult to like themselves. Therapy can give such children a second chance.

Georgie saw himself as reflected in my expression as evoking tenderness and worth taking seriously. He therefore felt himself to be good. (Reid, 1990, p49)

Therapy for children who have been given up for adoption

Year in, year out, some adopted children desperately seek love and approval from their birth parent, who, because of their *own* childhood, is unable to give it. And yet the child clings to the hope that some day this parent will love him. His self-worth hangs on his rejecting parent. It is a terrible plight. Such a child can always benefit from therapy: he needs help to mourn the reality that what he yearns for so desperately is unlikely ever to happen, and then to move on to people who can take pleasure and delight in him. He needs help to turn away from his birth parent (who has turned away from him), to the more benign world beyond.

RECOMMENDED READING

Armstrong-Perlman EM, 1991, 'The Allure of the Bad Object', *Free Associations* 2 (3) part 23, pp343–56.

Berke JH, 1989, *The Tyranny of Malice,* Simon & Schuster, London.

Berne E, 1964, *Games People Play*, Grove Press, New York.

Bloch D, 1978, *So The Witch Won't Eat Me: Fantasy and the Child's Fear of Infanticide*, Grove Press, New York.

Blume ES, 1990, *Secret Survivors: Uncovering Incest and its After-effects in Women*, John Wiley, Chichester/New York.

Glen M, 1990, *Ruby,* Red Fox/Hutchinson, London. (For children who need to feel special – a book about a teddy.)

Hendrix H, 1993, *Getting the Love You Want*, Pocket Books, London/New York.

Miller A, 1987, *For Your Own Good: The Roots of Violence in Child-Rearing*, Virago, London. (For children who have been physically abused in childhood.)

Miller A, 1991, *Thou Shalt Not Be Aware: Society's Betrayal of the Child*, Pluto, London. (First published 1981.) (For children who have been sexually abused in childhood.)

Rand A, 1964, *The Virtue of Selfishness*, Signet, New York.

Rowe D, 1988, *The Successful Self*, Fontana, London.

Schoenewolf G, 1991, *The Art of Hating*, Jason Aronson, Northvale, NJ.

Stewart I & Joines V, 1987, *T.A. Today*, Lifespace, Nottingham.

Terr L, 1994, *Unchained Memories: True Stories of Traumatic Memories, Lost and Found*, Basic Books, New York.

BIBLIOGRAPHY

Ammons AR, 1993, *Garbage,* WW Norton, New York.

Andersen HC, 1996, *A Treasury of Stories from Hans Christian Andersen,* Kingfisher, London.

Armstrong-Perlman EM, 1995, 'Psychosis: The Sacrifice that Fails?', Ellwood J (ed), *Psychosis: Understanding and Treatment,* Jessica Kingsley, London, pp93–102.

Balint E, 1993, *Before I Was I: Psychoanalysis and the Imagination* (Mitchell J & Parsons M, eds), Free Association Books, London.

Berke JH, 1987, 'Shame and Envy', Nathanson DL (ed) *The Many Faces of Shame,* Guildford Press, London/New York, pp318–34.

Berke JH, 1989, *The Tyranny of Malice,* Simon & Schuster, London.

Berne E, 1964, *Games People Play*, Grove Press, New York.

Blume ES, 1990, *Secret Survivors: Uncovering Incest and its After-effects in Women*, John Wiley, Chichester/New York.

Buber M, 1958, *I and Thou* (Gregor Smith R trans), T&T Clark, Edinburgh. (First published 1937.)

Carroll L, 1970, *The Annotated Alice* (Gardner M ed) Penguin, London.

Casement P, 1990, *Further Learning from the Patient: The Analytic Space & Process*, Tavistock/Routledge, London.

Clarkson P, 1988, 'Ego State Dilemmas of Abused Children', *Transactional Analysis Journal* 18 (2), pp85–93.

Clarkson P, 1989, *Gestalt Counselling in Action*, Sage, London.

Damasio A, 1996, *The Feeling of What Happens*, Vintage, London.

Dickens C, 1995, *Great Expectations*, Penguin/Puffin, Harmondsworth. (First published 1861.)

Dostoevsky FM, 1991, *Notes from the Underground* (Kentish J trans), Oxford University Press, Oxford. (Original work published 1864.)

Drabble M, 1996, 'Umbrella of Darkness', Dunn S, Morrison B & Roberts M (eds), *Mind Readings – Writers' Journeys Through Mental States*, Minerva, London, pp91–5.

Eliot L, 1999, *What's Going on in There? How the Brain and Mind Develop in the First Five Years of Life*, Bantam, New York.

Erikson EH, 1977, *Childhood and Society*, Triad/Granada, London. (Original work published 1950.)

Fairbairn WRD, 1952a, 'The Repression and the Return of Bad Objects (with special reference to the "War Neuroses")', in *Psychoanalytic Studies of the Personality,* Tavistock/Routledge, London, pp59–81. (First published in 1943.)

Fairbairn WRD, 1952b, 'Endopsychic Structure Considered in Terms of Object-Relationships', *Psychoanalytic Studies of the Personality*, Tavistock/Routledge, London, pp82–136. (First published in 1944.)

Feinstein L, 2001, 'The Impact of Children's Self-esteem on their Education and Employment Prospects', paper given at The Institute for Public Policy Research 2001 (Mainstreaming Mental Health in Schools).

Fenichel O, 1945, *The Psychoanalytic Theory of Neurosis*, Routledge, London.

Freud S, 1979, 'Repression', *On Metapsychology: The Theory of Psychoanalysis*, Vol 11 of *The Penguin Freud Library*, Richards A & Strachey J (eds); trans J Strachey, Penguin, Harmondsworth, pp139–57. (First published in 1915.)

Fromm E, 1973, *The Anatomy of Human Destructiveness*, Cape, London.

Gendlin ET, 1978, *Focussing*, Bantam/Everest, New York.

Gilbert P, 1992, *Depression: The Evolution & Powerlessness*, Guildford Press, New York.

Glouberman D, 1989, *Life Choices & Life Changes through Imagework: The Art of Developing Personal Vision*, Unwin, London.

Graves R, 1964, *The Greek Myths*, Penguin, Harmondsworth.

Greenberg JR & Mitchell SA, 1983, *Object Relations in Psychoanalytic Theory*, Harvard University Press, London/Cambridge, MA.

Hinshelwood RD, 1989, *A Dictionary of Kleinian Thought*, Free Association Books, London.

Home Office, The, 1994, 'Homicide Statistics: "Offences Currently Recorded as Homicide by Age of Victim"', *Criminal Statistics England and Wales 1994*, HMSO, London.

Horney K, 1977, *The Neurotic Personality of Our Time*, Routledge, London. (Original work published 1937.)

Hughes D, 1998, *Building the Bonds of Attachment*, Jason Aronson, New Jersey.

Hughes T, 1995, *New Selected Poems 1957–1994*, Faber & Faber, London.

Hycner R, 1993, *Between Person and Person: Toward a Dialogical Psychotherapy,* Gestalt Journal Press.

Izard CE & Schwartz GM, 1986, 'Patterns of Emotion in Depression', Rutter M, Izard CE & Read PB (eds), *Depression in Young People: Developmental and Clinical Perspectives*, Guildford Press, New York.

Jackson M & Williams P, 1994, *Unimaginable Storms: A Search for Meaning in Psychosis*, Karnac, London.

Jeffers S, 1992, *Dare to Connect*, Piatkus, London.

Jeffers S, 1995, 'On relationships', *The Oprah Winfrey Show*, Channel 4 TV, 9 September.

Jenner S, 1999, *The Parent-Child Game,* Bloomsbury, London.

Johnson SM, 1994, *Character Styles,* Norton, New York.

Jung CG, 1982, *Aspects of the Feminine*, Princeton University Press, Princeton.

Kahn MMR, 1991, *Between Therapist and Client: The New Relationship*, WH Freeman, New York.

Keenan B, 1992, *An Evil Cradling*, Vintage, London.

Klein M, 1946, *Envy and Gratitude: And Other Works 1946–1963*, Vintage, London.

Klein M, 1988, 'The Psychotherapy of the Psychoses', *Love, Guilt and Reparation and Other Works 1921–1945*, Virago, London. (First published in 1930.)

Kohut H, 1984, *How Does Analysis Cure?* University of Chicago, London/ Chicago.

Lewis, 1987, 'Shame the Narcisstic Personality', Nathanson DL (ed), *The Many Faces of Shame*, Guildford Press, New York.

Massie H, 2002, 'The Relationship Between Parent-Infant Interaction, Child Trauma and Subsequent Mental Health: Results of a Longitudinal Study From Birth to Age Thirty', lecture at The Centre for Child Mental Health, 31 May.

Massie H, 2003, *Lives Across Time*, Henry Holt Co, New York.

McKee D, 1996, *Not Now Bernard*, Red Fox/Random House, London.

Miller A, 1987, *The Drama of Being a Child: And The Search for the True Self*, (Ward R trans), Virago, London.

Mitchell SA, 1988, *Relational Concepts in Psychoanalysis*, Harvard University Press, Cambridge, MA.

Mitchell SA, 1995, *Relationality: From Attachment to Intersubjectivity (Relational Perspectives)*, Analytic Press, New Jersey.

Montagu A, 1971, *Touching: The Human Significance of the Skin*, Harper & Row, London.

Moore T, 1992, *Care of the Soul: A Guide for Cultivating Depth and Sacredness in Everyday Life*, HarperCollins, New York.

Moore T, 1994, *Soul Mates*, HarperCollins, New York.

Murray L, 1988, 'Effects of Postnatal Depression on Infant Development: Direct Studies of Early Mother-Infant Reactions', Kumar R and Brockington IF (eds), *Motherhood and Mental Illness 2: Causes and Consequences*, Wright, London/Boston, pp159–90.

Nathanson DL, 1987, 'A Timetable for Shame', Nathanson DL (ed) *The Many Faces of Shame*, Guildford Press, London/New York, pp1–63.

Neruda P, 1969, *Twenty Love Poems and a Song of Despair,* Cape, London.

Orbach S, 1994, *What's Really Going On Here?* Virago, London.

Panksepp J, 1998, *Affective Neuroscience: The Foundations of Human and Animal Emotions*, Oxford University Press, Oxford.

Pinter H, 1991, *Collected Poems and Prose*, Faber & Faber, London.

Plath S, 1981, *Collected Poems*, Faber & Faber, London.

Polster E, 1987, *Every Person's Life is Worth a Novel*, Norton, New York.

Reid S, 1990, 'The Importance of Beauty in the Psychoanalytic Experience', *Journal of Child Psychotherapy* 16 (1), pp29-52. (Originally given at a study weekend of the Association of Child Psychotherapists, March 1987.)

Rosenfeld H, 1965, *Psychotic States: A Psychoanalytical Approach*, Maresfield Library, London.

Rowan J, 1986, *Ordinary Ecstasy: Humanistic Psychology in Action*, Routledge & Kegan Paul, London.

Rowe D, 1988, *The Successful Self,* Fontana, London.

Rowe CE & MacIsaac DS, 1989, *Empathic Attunement: The 'Technique' of Psychoanalytic Self Psychology*, Jason Aronson, Northvale, NJ.

Sartre J-P, 1956, *Being and Nothingness* (Barnes HE trans), Philosophical Library, New York. (Original work, *L'Etre et le Neant* published 1943.)

Schneider CD, 1987, 'A Mature Sense of Shame', Nathanson DL (ed) *The Many Faces of Shame*, Guildford Press, London/New York, pp194–213.

Shakespeare W, 1994, *The Complete Works of William Shakespeare*, HarperCollins, London.

Siegel D, 1999, *The Developing Mind*, Guildford Press, New York.

Solomon I, 1985, 'On Feeling Hopeless', *Psychoanalytic Review* 72 (1), pp55–69.

Steiner J, 1977, *The Original Warm Fuzzy Tale*, Jalmar Press, California.

Stern DN, 1990, *Diary of a Baby – What Your Child Sees, Feels and Experiences*, Basic Books, New York.

Stolorow RD, Brandchaft B & Atwood GE, 1987, 'Affects and Self-objects', *Psychoanalytic Treatment: An Intersubjective Approach* (Vol 8 of *Psychoanalytic Inquiry* series), Analytic Press, Hillsdale, NJ/London, pp66–87.

Thrail E, 1994, *Retrospect: The Story of an Analysis*, Quartet, London.

Watzlawick P, 1983, *The Situation is Hopeless, But Not Serious*, Norton, London/New York.

Whitman W, 1995, *Leaves of Grass*, Penguin Classics, Harmondsworth. (Original work published 1855.)

Williamson M, 1992, *A Return to Love*, Random House, New York.

Winnicott DW, 1965, *The Maturational Process and the Facilitating Environment,* Hogarth, London.

Yalom ID, 1980, *Existential Psychotherapy*, Basic Books, New York.